Dear Dev[...],
   Here's to a great
2024 Season.
   This is our story. We
hope you enjoy the read.
   Go Noles!

   [signature] & [signature]

Married
To It

By
Bob and Gail
Knight

How An Entrepreneurial Couple Built a Photography Empire
By Investing in Their Customers, Staff, and Each Other

First edition November 2019
ISBN 978-0-578-60415-2
Published by Married To It, LLC

Cover, Jacket & Title Page Photos by Tony Ivory
Back Cover Photo by Tony Ivory
copyright ©2019
Photo Designs by Ivory Fine Art Portraits
Printed by DeHarts Media Services

We dedicate this book to our three boys who put up with a lot.

Timothy Fitzgerald Knight
Daniel Brock Knight
Thomas Gifford Knight

Contents

Foreword

When friends and colleagues first mentioned the idea of writing a book to Bob and me, I don't think either of us were that interested in it. We were in the process of selling our stake in the latest, and most profitable, iteration of Bob Knight Photo and were focused on finishing that deal, then booking our retirement travel plans. But trusted protégés like Michelle Jagers, Anne Munson and Jenn Vestal pressed home the point — this story, our story, is one of love, laughter, learning, but also significant professional growth, and, happily, financial success.

What follows in this book is the story of how a boy from Miami and a girl from Ohio met at Florida State University in Tallahassee, Florida and teamed up to take over the world — or at least a decent portion of its photography market.

Between 35 years of marriage and four years before of dating, that's nearly four decades as partners in every sense of the word (not to mention 28 years of parenting). We worked together, raised three amazing young men and somehow figured out a way to not kill each other in the process.

People say to me all the time, "I could never work with my spouse."

Well it hasn't been easy.

I confess that I almost offed him a couple of times. We developed some hardcore rules to live by which we still follow today.

Rule 1: Plans don't change unless both parties know about it. This isn't hard to follow now with the technical advancements that have come along in the past 40 years, but if my phone dies and he can't reach me, I still know he will be where he said he would be, waiting. (Maybe not so patiently but at least he will be there.)

Rule 2. No talking business at home or at a restaurant without explicit permission from the other partner. This was a big one. Without it we would have talked shop nonstop. I'm pretty sure that would have sunk us in the early days.

Rule 3. Bob is allowed to be an asshole 10% of the time, but I get to pick the occasion.

I learned early on that Bob could be a real asshole. Sometimes it was embarrassing, even if it was borne out of his own passion for customer service that I think was directly responsible for the success of our business.

So, I made the rule. I also knew that Bob does not like being at a counter: rental car, hotel, and especially airline counters. So, I do all the "checking in" while he paces in the background not far away, waiting for my subtle nod indicating I'm not getting what I want, and he needs to step in. He steps forward and simply says "What seems to be the problem?"

I'm happy to say, over the past four decades, whatever problems we have had, we have been able to overcome. And mostly without Bob having to be a "ten-percenter."

It's been an amazing ride, living the American dream, and enjoying that sense of gratification that comes with reaching the highest levels of an industry. We shared ownership of what became one of the largest photographic organizations in the world. And we did it all with our sons who came along for the ride. Our success has allowed us (our kids, personal family and work family) to pursue our true passion: traveling the world.

Yes, we vacation together too. There is no one I like to travel with more than Bobby Knight. But no matter where we go, we are also very happy to return to where it all started.

We met at FSU in the Fall of 1979. He was famous among the sororities there and I was a little intimidated at first. But once I got to know him I decided he was "kinda handsome but oh so hyper." He was all over the place. I'd say he had too many irons in the fire but it was really more like too many irons in too many fires. He was trying to maintain his fledgling sorority business, grow into other markets and take classes to finish his degree.

I could tell his company needed some basic structure (other than managing from his personal checkbook). And when I asked him when he was going to graduate, and he told me 1983 or 1984 (was he on the seven or eight year plan?). I knew that something needed to change if we were going to make it.

So, I jumped into the deep end of the pool. I outlined a plan for him to graduate with me in 1982 (he beat me to it and graduated in Summer 1981) and I started making changes to how he ran his business.

The changes were subtle at first. His Greek business was running very well by the time I came along, but I saw right away the real potential in the graduation market. He worked really hard to make sure his proofs from the weekend's sorority parties were in the houses before Chapter meetings on Monday nights. He knew speed of proof delivery mattered in that market and it really needed to matter in the grad market. So, I told him he needed to run two shifts in the office to make sure proofs were mailed within 48 hours from the ceremony (my first metric). He said "That's a great idea. Why don't you run it?" I thought he was kidding but he was not. So, in the summer of 1980, I ran the night shift from 5 pm until 1 am Monday through Friday. During the day I took my summer schedule of accounting classes.

You know what, it worked! Sales increased almost 25% over the previous graduation season. Something bigger happened that year, but it took a while for either of us to realize it. This was long before proposals of marriage or commitments into the future, but there was a synergy between us.

At the young ages of 23 and 20 our relationship was already unique. We respected each other and each other's strengths and abilities. Bob was the vision guy and I was the one who took care of the details. I didn't mess with his growth plan for expanding into other markets and he let me change everything else.

Slowly but steadily, what was now "our business" was

growing, and we weren't just surviving, but truly thriving. Bob was implementing a culture of sales and service with our staff that would set an industry standard. And I was focused on creating and improving new metrics that would allow us to be not only efficient, but innovative and cost effective. And it worked — better than either of us could ever have imagined.

We see all that with hindsight now, but it was true, and it was tested all the time. Our trust and respect for each other helped us survive the lean years, and there were some. It helped us make tough decisions when we were betting our future on new potential opportunities. And I am happy in the knowledge that not only could none of this have happened without me, but that I married a man who knows it, and brags about it.

The person we hired to help us write this book wasn't smart enough to figure out how to use both our voices as the narrative for this effort. So, after this Foreword, Bob's will be the perspective from which our story is told.

But make no mistake, this is our story.

Bob's drive to win and relentless commitment to customer service helped bring in the business, and my focus on numbers and systems made sure we maximized our successes. We were, and are, a terrific team.

Being Married to It means being fully committed to each other in every pursuit. It just so happens that our pursuit was our marriage, our business, and our children. I'm proud to have played a vital role in all three.

I'll let Bob take it from here. But if he starts getting out of hand, I won't hesitate to jump back in.

I've done it before. ~~Gail Knight

Introduction

Images of Success

As the founder and principal partner of the largest event photography company in the country, you possess a good number of skills. You have to learn to recognize opportunity when it presents itself. You have to learn customer management and how to keep them happy when something has gone wrong. You have to know how to identify talent and then train that talent to execute the mission of the company. You have to cultivate and then project and protect the values of the business into and from anyone you come in contact with.

You also have to learn how to talk your way into places.

I recently talked my way into a high school graduation, like I'd done a thousand times before.

Graduations, after all, are what have made my and my wife's company, Bob Knight Photo, the multimillion-dollar business it became. In 2005, the year before private equity firms would seek to buy our business and merge it with competitors, we photographed 5 percent of the 5.7 million high school, college, and professional graduates in the country. That's more than 300,000 graduates and over 1 million images per year.

But I'm not photographing anyone tonight. I don't own the
company anymore.

So, while I am no longer officially affiliated with the company
that my wife, Gail and I built, I still like to check in on things from
time to time, just to make sure things are running smoothly. I mean,
Gail and I are still happily married. But my first wife, my first real love,
was that company. The collection of people that company, Bob Knight
Photo, employed became my surrogate family. And together with that
family, we didn't just build a multimillion-dollar business, we pioneered
an industry. That industry, the capture and delivery of graduation
photographs, became my first child. And on this night, I'm here to
check on my child.

So when I pull up to the back gates of the Donald L. Tucker
Civic Center at Florida State University and tell the security officer I'm
with the photographers, he nods knowingly and asks for my name.

Of course, my name won't be on his clipboard.

"My name won't be on your list," I inform the heavy-set
gentleman in the yellow jacket. "I'm here to do a quality check."

He looks me over, seeing an older white guy in a suit driving a
Lexus, gives it a second of thought, then waves me through.

Security breached.

That's the biggest thing to keep in mind if you ever walk into
a place you shouldn't be: act like you own the place. It's a lesson I've
learned many times. It's sort of how I built my business. So tonight, here
I go again, walking in through the back door of the Civic Center, home
to graduations for seven area high schools and two colleges.

Walking through the door, there is an additional layer of security—a couple of police officers plus event-specific staff there to monitor the rear entrance. But I'm strolling in like I have a thousand times before, even though this time I am most definitely not really supposed to be here. But my child is calling.

I nod to the cops and the staff, then proceed toward the corridor that opens up to the larger arena floor. On stage, the school officials are settling into their spots, preparing to endure the next three hours of pleasantries and platitudes along with hyped-up high-schoolers and their cheering families in the crowd.

For their part, the students sit dutifully in the rows in front of the stage, some of them arranging their robes and regalia for their pre-graduation selfie. But my eyes, as always in these settings, aren't on the graduates or school administration. They're on the subtly taped spots on stage, where principals know to stand as they shake hands and hand out diplomas. That's where the students will stop and pose for the photographers, strategically positioned to snap the most important moment many of these students have had in life up to this point.

My eyes then look behind the stage, to the small curtained-off closet where the photographers and their gear sit, preparing to harvest the thousands of images from this event alone. I swing by to see if I know any of them. The team captain is Matt Schnipert, the man I trained twenty years ago, who has a full-time job as a teacher but still leads photo teams for extra money.

I scan the crowd, where the parents and extended family, friends, and well-wishers await their chance to hoot and holler when the name of their celebrated graduate is called. Their cheers are among the sweetest sounds you can ever hear. And for me, the most profitable. Each one of those kids walking across the stage, and their families in the stands, plus their relations across the world who couldn't make it to the event that night, are potential customers of mine. Each stop at the tape on the stage, each choreographed pose and shake with a principal, each stop along the student's way to becoming a high school graduate, is potential revenue for me and my company. For my family.

But now the real work begins.

While the ceremony concludes and the graduation caps are thrown in the air, the photographers' cases are closed, and their flash cards with the images are loaded onto laptops, every piece of equipment having a place, and every digital image having a code.

That's how we designed it.

I don't stick around to watch what happens next because I know it all too well.

They'll hustle the equipment and images back to the office, also located in Tallahassee, where the work of matching the image to the graduate, the picture with the customer, will begin. Within forty-eight hours, those proud parents will get to see a proof of what their child looked like in such accomplished splendor. And then hopefully decide to spend $7.99 on a 5 x 7 or purchase all the images as a package. After all, at this school, thanks to Gail, I know that we averaged around twenty dollars per graduate photographed.

I slip out the back as the ceremony breaks up with hugs between the students and families and more photographs for all involved, using the ubiquitous high-resolution cameras masquerading as smart phones that nearly all attendees possess.

I am getting out at the right time.

The images taken this night won't belong to my company and won't benefit my business. Gail and I sold our shares in 2018, leaving me, for the first time in forty years, with no vested interest in graduation season. So you can maybe understand why I am having a hard time letting it go.

In just Florida, Bob Knight Photo owned the contracts for 157 of the 159 state colleges and university graduation ceremonies, as well as nearly 75 percent of all the high schools. We were earning two-thirds of our $9 million in revenue from Florida schools with California providing the remainder. We would eventually merge with our competitors and have a larger national footprint with contracts in every region of the country, producing 55 million images last year. But we were only able to do that because of the financial and logistical success of BKP.

Breaking into a high school graduation ceremony certainly isn't the first rule Gail or I broke along the way. I've stolen ideas from corporate titans. I've given things away to customers at a time when all the corporate brain trusts and studies said to focus on profit. Gail and I hired bartenders and dental hygienists and put them to work as photographers. I even slept with a subordinate. (Spoiler alert — it was Gail.)

You can break rules on your way to the top, but it's important to follow some as well. This book is about Gail's and my story — what we did, how we did it, and the mistakes and successes we had along the way. But the first lesson, as I now drive past the security guard at the gate and give him a wave, is to always dress and act like you own the place. You'll be amazed at the places you can go. I know I am.

Gail and I have been very fortunate, and, perhaps more importantly, we have been lucky enough to take advantage of opportunities when they came along. A lot of those opportunities included the ability to be surrounded by a great staff of over 1,400, including part-time photographers, a killer support team of professionals, and dedicated suppliers who, in the early years, mostly just tolerated me as a brash upstart who liked to talk a lot.

But none of the success that Bob Knight Photo had would have happened if it hadn't been for a bounced check from Alpha Gamma Delta. For Gail, as their treasurer, it was horrifying. But for me, it was the greatest form of nonpayment in the history of corporate America.

This book is my story. Our story. It is the story, however unlikely, of a kid from Miami who comes to FSU in 1975 and, along with his eventual partner, seizes on a long shot opportunity at age nineteen and somehow takes that idea and company nationwide thirty years later. I still can't believe how far we've come. Especially when you consider how I got started.

ONE

Staging

Building an Empire One Picture at a Time

S uccessful people who reflect on their profitable careers and say something like, "I'm lucky to be here" seem trite and clichéd. And as much as possible in this book, I'm going to try to be honest and authentic. So how about this—as a teenaged entrepreneur who, along with my future wife and business partner, built the largest event photography company in the world, I'm lucky I didn't go to prison.

Tallahassee, Florida, is a good place to be most of the time, but especially in the fall, and 1976 was no exception. Rosalyn Carter would campaign at the Capitol building with then Governor Reubin Askew as part of the buildup to that November's election, and a new football coach named Bobby Bowden was getting ready for his first season in charge of Florida State. And I, a heretofore overconfident and driven college sophomore, was sitting in my apartment on the edge of FSU's campus, staring at tens of thousands of pictures I had taken the previous week and paid for by writing a $15,000 check to the federal government with no money to back it up.

As the enormity of the volume of pictures I needed to sort, catalog, deliver and collect payment for began to rise in my mind, I felt another type of pain and stress from a different part of my body.

My stomach was growling—I hadn't eaten anything in a couple days.

My pantry was as empty as my one-bedroom apartment was full of pictures: prints of sorority girls at any number of rush events from the days before were stacked on top of my kitchen counter, couch, television, and even the bathroom sink. The only thing edible in my possession was one remaining can of Chef Boyardee Ravioli.

So I sat down on the floor of my apartment with my can and a spoon and ate my dinner as the faces of the women of Florida State's Greek community looked on. Their looks of silent revelry only underscored my own desperation.

I sat, ate, and wondered. How the hell did I end up here?

Growing up in Miami, photography had been a bit of a hobby for me, and I had learned my way around an SLR camera at a fairly young age, but I never thought for a moment that I would end up using photography as a vehicle for a career. In high school, I was very involved in speech and debate and student government. I worked for a semester my junior year as a congressional page in Washington, D.C. In my senior year, I would even become student body president. I had always been polished and poised around older people of authority, and my plan was to go to FSU, find a means to pay my way through school, graduate with a strong liberal arts degree, and head to law school and probably a career in politics.

So in the fall of 1975, I rumbled up to Tallahassee in my nine-year-old 1966 Impala SS. By the time I arrived, I had already arranged for a part-time job working for an old friend from my high school. The job was party pic photography for fraternities and sororities. I would go out on Thursday, Friday, and Saturday nights and take semi-posed pictures of friends having fun in their various stages of inebriation. The job paid by the roll of film, about $5.00 for every thirty-six pictures taken. That was a good deal for me because I could shoot pictures really fast back then, really work the room, getting as many of the attendees involved as possible. After all, the more people who were in the pictures, the more potential customers you had.

Party pics were becoming wildly popular around the country but were just getting started as a viable service in Tallahassee. My friend from high school, Mark McCarl, who was a college senior when I was a freshman, only had a handful of sororities under contract in 1975, but I thought I saw the beginning of a cultural phenomenon.

I decided that this was just the vehicle I needed to pay my way through school, and in the summer of 1976, I offered to buy the business for $1,000. Technically, all I bought was "goodwill" and his signature on a non-compete agreement because there were no real assets and the contracts had expired. But I didn't have $1,000, so he took a promise from me that I'd pay some day, hopefully before Christmas that year. I wonder if he really ever thought he would see a dime. To get ready for the fall season, the coming Rush, and Bid Day for sororities at FSU, I went to every house and offered enhanced services for photography, touting my ability to cover each day's events and selling a vision for a new tradition of group pictures for each pledge class. Just about every house signed up. I had sixteen signed contracts in my possession, and I had increased the value of the business within a matter of a few months. There was just one problem. I had no means of fulfilling what I had just sold.

So, young entrepreneur, let that be the first big lesson from this book: before selling something, make sure you have capacity to pull it off.

And to be clear, when I say I had no means of pulling it off, I mean literally no means. I had no photographers, no equipment, no retainer fees (it was all on speculation), no marketing system, and no packaging or delivery system on that scale.

I needed a lot of things. But mostly, I needed money. So I did what most college kids do when they mess up and need some help getting out of a jam. I begged my parents for help.

I drove that yellow Impala back down to Miami and had a long talk with my dad, who I'm sure was relatively horrified with what I had just done and what I was saying I was about to do.

"What about school?" he asked.

"Oh, don't worry, I'm still a student," I reassured him. (Spoiler alert—it would take me six years to actually graduate.)

"What about getting a real job?" my mother wanted to know.

"Oh, of course, I still plan on getting a law degree," I replied. (I didn't, though several months later, because of my professional overextension and bad check writing, I feared I would be in need of an actual lawyer.)

Somehow, Dad agreed to loan me $5,000 to get started, which he was able to do by putting up physical stock certificates in Knight

Ridder, which owned the *Miami Herald,* his employer, for collateral. By the time Fall Rush rolled around, I had hired a bunch of people, bought hundreds of rolls of film, and gotten as many used cameras I could find. And the $5,000 was gone. I was broke again. So how was I going to be able to fulfill orders, print, and pay for the final pictures? I was just nineteen, had no credit cards and no real access to more cash. So what was my plan? Well, in 1976, the most common form of payment was writing a check. So I realized writing checks allowed me the time to collect the receivables and put the money in the account before the check would clear. It could work, but I had to be creative, and it would all be about timing.

My photofinishing house, Candid Color Systems in Oklahoma City, was smart enough not to accept my check. So I decided I would have it all shipped COD (Cash on Delivery) through the post office and write the federal government the bad checks. I figured that if I was going to kite worthless checks, I was going to do it with style points. But the post office would only take a business check for shipments that were Cash on Delivery, or COD. (For the millennials reading this, that means we didn't have to pay for it until it arrived.) So I convinced my bank to allow me to put my licensed business name at the top of the check and list a local PO box. Then I ordered the checks in a really large size. These were enormous checks that came in a big book and looked like they would be attached to a legitimate, going concern.

So the execution of the first Bid Day was a smashing success. I, along with my team of newly hired photographers, took tens of thousands of pictures and received $40,000 worth of orders, too. All I had to do was print the pictures, deliver, collect the money, and make a deposit. My plan was going to work.

On the day the pictures arrived COD, I went down to the post office and wrote a $15,000 worthless check to the United States government via the Postal Service, and I was actually somewhat surprised when they handed me six large boxes, full of Bid Day pictures.

When I say the check was worthless, I mean literally worthless. There was no money in that account, just pennies, really.

When I got home to my one-bedroom apartment, I stacked up all the pictures on top of every piece of furniture I owned, or was renting, and contemplated how to deliver all that product in time to make a deposit before the check would clear.

Physically seeing the volume of my responsibility, I knew I had screwed up. And could be facing serious jail time. So I got out my ravioli and started to think.

I knew I couldn't get it all done and started to panic a little bit. So I sat there on the floor with a spoon and a can in front of my coffee table and reconciled to myself that tomorrow I was going to jail for perhaps multiple federal crimes.

It was then that I made one of the most important decisions of my life. I picked up the phone and started calling my friends. My first call was to my friend Joanne Amos, a good friend who was an excellent organizer and was in the Kappa Delta sorority.

"Give me six to eight girls who will come over because they're nice people," I begged. Combining an alluring mix of desperation and financial incentive, I was begging for help and offering them a job.

Before long, the Kappa Delta cavalry arrived.

Along with other friends and neighbors, my first team of employees stayed up all night with me to get the orders organized and packaged for individual delivery. Over the next thirty-six hours, we had delivered all the pictures, collected the outstanding balances, and made the deposits to the bank just in time for my check to clear the post office. I still feel some regret for the degree of real tenacity from my Accounts Receivable Department (that was me) that day. I was pretty aggressive with the treasurers of my new sorority customers. But damn, we got it done.

I still didn't have a healthy business at that point, but at least I stayed out of jail. It would be another two years before I would reach a positive cash flow. But the foundation, flawed as it was, for what Bob Knight Photo would become had been laid. And for the rest of its existence, that company, with my name, would continue to employ my friends and neighbors, and their friends and cousins, and anyone else in the network I thought could get the job done. I knew I was starting a business. But I began to realize that with my collection of friends and neighbors turned employees helping with each hayride, Sadie Hawkins Dance, and Spring formal, I was also starting a family.

Over the next few months, my new family and I successfully executed each Greek event as part of the expanded service I had pitched to them that summer. The results were great for revenue but terrible for my grades. So, wanting to strike while the iron was hot and also provide a workable rationale for my academic failings, I immediately expanded the party pic business to five other Florida universities which had active

Greek systems. It would mean a lot of travel for me and my employees in Tallahassee. But hey—I had just avoided prison. Why not double down? Plus, by sorting and delivering the pictures from the Tallahassee events in such a quick turnaround time, we had essentially developed the system I knew could be used for other clients.

Then, just six months later, I had another great idea. I had heard of a photography firm in Missouri with a similar business model as mine that photographed graduates as they received their diplomas. What a great idea! Doesn't everyone want to record the moment of walking across the stage to receive the hard-earned diploma? But you just can't get that picture from the bleachers, and it wasn't being done anywhere in Florida by anyone. And, as it turns out, for good reason. Taking pictures of hundreds or thousands of graduates just seconds after one another, then figuring out how to get those pictures to each individual graduate, along with, of course, collecting their payment information in a short amount of time, wasn't easy. In fact, it was a real logistical nightmare.

I knew for it to work I would have to develop and lock down some workflow systems, devise a sequence for names and images, acquire home addresses, and convince someone to give me a shot. Then if it worked, I could, in theory, bring this service to all Florida schools. Why wouldn't both high schools and colleges be interested? All I would need to do is find just one client in each of Florida's largest counties and expand from there.

So in January of 1977, I put on my suit and made my way to Leon High School in downtown Tallahassee to ask for an appointment with the principal, Mike Conley. A gracious and cordial man, he immediately met with me without reservation, even though I was just twenty years old, and he knew I was there to pitch a business opportunity. I guess I was convincing enough, and he quickly agreed the service was needed, and that he'd like to be my first customer. I remember him saying, "Let's do it."

Leaving Leon that day, I had a brief moment of sales euphoria, but then standing there on those great front steps of the main building, I had one of those queasy feelings. It occurred to me that I had done it again. I had no idea of how in the world I was going to photograph Leon's graduation ceremony. Taking a picture of all 400 seniors in intervals of two seconds each, then identifying each individual? Plus the cameras were a little delicate for that volume, and the flash units could not recycle fast enough to keep up with the pace. I would have to get all that figured out plus a new marketing plan since now I was going after parents of high school kids who would want them looking serious and scholarly, exactly the opposite of the demographic and vibe I was used to for the party pics. Walking down Leon's steps towards the parking lot, I wanted another can of ravioli.

At least this time I knew who to call, even if I had no idea how we were going to do it. My intrepid team of part-time twenty-year-olds and I got to work on solving an engineering issue that literally no one in the industry had figured out.

From a field operations perspective, there were two issues which had to be solved. First, how would we handle the logistics of actually taking the pictures of all 400 graduates at the moment they received their diploma, in intervals of two seconds each, without stopping, and without missing anyone. It was, to put it mildly, a logistical nightmare under the best of circumstances. In fact, it still is. And by the way, it all had to be done in a way that we could sequence pictures so that they matched the students' names to their faces. Then, we had to acquire all the parents' addresses and match those to the names and faces, all in the context of a ceremony where the last thing anyone is focused on is giving these strange college kids with cameras their contact information.

The second issue was more technical but just as crucial. The ideal electronic flashes, called strobes, did not exist in 1976–77. So we didn't have the ideal equipment which could light the shot adequately, then recharge in time to do it all again in the next two seconds. I know people must think of the time before digital cameras as the Dark Ages, but in this case inadequate light was an actual problem.

So now we were looking at a new marketing plan, new systems, new equipment, and probably more money than I had. I knew all this going in and had been in stages of processing all this for a few months.

Logistically, we were going to need to rehearse everything. We needed a plan for staging and choreography. We needed to work with Mr. Conley so we were in the right position for the best angle for the handshake shot. A few adjustments in school tradition needed to be made. And Leon was willing to, as I liked to say, help us help them.

Now, if you've ever been to a graduation ceremony, you know that the highlight is when the speeches stop and graduates are lined up to have their names read and parade across the stage, shaking hands with multiple greeters and receiving their degrees. But from our point of view, it's relentless. They just keep coming, like a Zulu attack on my position. Joanne Cox, an administrator at Mosley High School, aptly quipped to me, during her rehearsal, that, "Passing out diplomas at graduation is like giving birth. Once it begins, there's no way to stop it."

Amen to that.

The point is that the only way to survive and properly execute a graduation ceremony shoot is if everything is in place, and everyone knows the plan. And there has to be a backup plan if something goes wrong. For us, that meant identical backup cameras on stage, ready to fire. So through the spring of 1977, we worked hard to figure all that out.

The other issue of an efficient, reliable strobe was more daunting, but my intrepid young team and I got to work. Because of the outdoor setting at night, studio lighting was out of the question. We needed the same portability of equipment we used for party pics. So all three models we tested used AA batteries, which didn't last very long and proved to have a very slow recycle time. It was also very expensive. In the first few years of operation, we spent more to purchase batteries than actual film. To solve that problem, we had turned to AC adapters for our portable strobes. Yes, we plugged the strobes into the wall and fired off 500 flashes. Eventually, some of our units began to smoke and then melt. We had no way of measuring amps or volts. So now, although we had terrific recycle time, we had too much power, which the strobes were not engineered to withstand. That's why in several tests we destroyed multiple units through overheating. Multiple times people would come to my apartment and be greeted by the inviting smell of burnt plastic and wires. I'm lucky no one called the cops on me over suspicions of bomb making or the like.

Finally, we figured out the right mix of adapters to outlets that would at least get us through this first ceremony in 1977. Or so we hoped.

Our homebrew solution in tow, we headed out to Capital Stadium, now known as Gene Cox Stadium, where Leon High conducted their ceremonies. With bright yellow extension cords stretched across the football field, the ceremony began, and we snapped our pictures, while holding our breath and saying our prayers, that the equipment would make it. By the end of the ceremony, our AC adapters and all of our Vivitar 352 strobes were smoking hot. But we did it. In just a couple of years, all that would change with new sources of battery power and the advance of newer models of strobes by two other competing brands, Metz and Sunpack. But we actually proved we could do it.

Fire hazards amidst a gathering of several hundred children and families aside, the graduation couldn't have gone better for us. It was not only a real success for our company, but it was also extremely popular among the parents. Mr. Conley wrote me a letter of recommendation, and a whole new photography segment was born.

Leaving the field that day, I was probably walking quite slowly because I was dragging extension cords, barely functioning lighting equipment, and mountains of other related gear. But in my mind, I was sprinting.

I knew we had just launched a new segment of business, and

there were as many potential clients as there were schools in the state. And Florida was a big state.

"I've got to run," I thought to myself. "It's a race." Luckily, I knew I had a couple things going for me. One was experience—I was already in the lead since I had just pulled off what, as far as I knew, was the first graduation ceremony photographs in the state. Two was geography.

Unlike a state like Ohio, which has potential competitors from every directional border, Florida is a peninsula. If I could suck up the business before competition came down from the north, I thought to myself, I could own the state.

So I started running.

In the previous two years, I had been traveling the state, cold calling universities and their sororities and fraternities. After that Leon graduation in 1977 though, I started adding high schools to the list. My goal was to see eleven schools in a day: three colleges and eight high schools.

Like I said, it was a race. And I was determined to win.

In the next year, we booked Mosley High School in Panama City, a school in St. Augustine, Daytona Beach, and one in Tampa. We also signed another school in Tallahassee: Godby High School. Godby's principal was a young man named Bill Montford, who would be as helpful as Mr. Conley was in our development.

Within two years, we had 166 client schools under contract, and the personal touch of going to meet every registrar or key school official in the state was paying off. Florida was growing, and my business was growing with it. For the state, that growth meant new schools. And new schools for the state meant new clients for me. I'd hear about new school openings from the assistant principals I was working with and would make it a point to be on the new principal's doorstep when construction was initiated. Often I'd have them signed as a client before construction was even finished and would even offer to take pictures of their opening ceremony for free.

By the time I met Gail, when she was treasurer at the Alpha Gamma Delta sorority, we were photographing over 50,000 Florida graduates each year, including our first university clients in UCF, FIU, and FSU. We were rolling, at least on paper. Or, rather, on the photo paper.

On the paper that mattered—bank statements and balance sheets—I was working my ass off to keep my head above water. We were rolling photo teams to every corner of the state, but we were also sending cash out as quickly as it was coming in. This was early 1978, before I met Gail. By 2005, with Gail by my side personally and professionally, that number would rise to 350,000 graduates in six states.

Yes, our company has taken a lot of photographs over the years. But some have proven to be more impactful than others.

TWO

A Page and a Cadet

From West Point and Capitol Hill to Florida State

The key to taking a great picture is timing. Everything needs to be lined up properly: the lighting, the expression on the subject's face, the background that hopefully conveys some type of contextual significance. As a photographer, you can be in the right place at the right time with your camera, but if some of the things you can't control aren't in place, the ceiling on the quality of your shot drops significantly.

Before both Gail and I arrived in Tallahassee, we were lucky to have had exposure to things that raised our ceilings significantly, and I think really put us in a position to be able to grow our business and reach the kinds of heights we did at relatively young ages.

I mean, I started traveling the state in the late 1970s as a twenty-year-old. So I would be approaching grown men and women, often times more than three times my age, and not only selling them my business services but essentially selling *myself.* I realize now that not every twenty-year-old would have been ready for that. And Gail, too, essentially became CFO and HR manager of Bob Knight Photo in her early twenties and led it to the $100 million company it would become.

Not bad for a couple of FSU grads.

The thing is, when we arrived in Tallahassee, we weren't your typical college freshmen. Like the best pictures, things happening in our backgrounds had prepared our pictures to be great. Before I got to FSU, I had the opportunity to serve as a page, and Gail had been a cadet.

I had the opportunity to go to Washington, D.C., as a congressional page in the fall of 1973. It was the beginning of my junior year in high school, but more importantly it was a time when the entire world was watching the drama surrounding the Nixon administration and Watergate.

I had always been a political junkie, and having the opportunity to go live in Washington as a page was a lifetime dream even though I was only sixteen years old.

As a high school freshman, I had approached my guidance counselor at Southwest Miami High School and asked how to go about becoming a page. I was told to meet my local congressman, and the best way to do that, as it happened, was to volunteer for his campaign. So at the august age of fourteen, I spent the afternoons of my ninth-grade year working for the campaign of Dante Fascell, a Democrat who represented my district in South Miami, manning phone banks and anything else the campaign would let an ambitious high school kid do. Because I was only 14, my mom would drop me off after school and pick me up about 8:00 pm. Talk about improving communications skills.

The thing is, I had been practicing the art of verbal persuasion for a long time. And I was good at it. Thanks in part to my speech and debate coaches—Sue Wilson at Southwest and Al Soriano at Rockway

Jr. High—I was highly ranked in Florida in the oratory and debate competitions which I participated in almost every weekend. By the end of high school, I could talk my way out of a paper bag.

By volunteering for the Fascell campaign, I secured his support for my participation as a congressional page. I actually applied for the position at age fifteen, but they wanted me to be at least sixteen as I would be on my own in our nation's capital. Three weeks into my junior year of high school, I got the call telling me I was selected, and that I could take the rest of my classes that fall at the Capitol Page School in the Library of Congress.

To say I was excited would be an understatement. I made travel arrangements, and, by October, I was living in Mrs. Thelma Smith's boarding house on the corner of NE 5th St. and A with two other pages, one from Louisiana and one from St. Louis. I was on the payroll as a federal employee working in the House of Representatives.

It was the first, and last, time I would live in government housing.

When I arrived at the Capitol on my first day, I was escorted into the office of William "Fishbait" Miller, the House Doorkeeper at the time. He briefed the group of new pages on the rules and handed out a sheet explaining proper etiquette on the House Floor and in the office buildings. Then he passed out assignments to each of us, designating which side of the aisle we would serve. Even though I was appointed by a Democratic Congressman (Fascell was actually chairman of the Committee on Foreign Relations at the time), Mr. Miller assigned me to the Republican side of the House. I was devastated. You should know that, at that time, the Democrats had an enormous majority in the House. I think the ratio was something like 345 Democrats to 90 Republicans. The number of pages on each side was split by the same ratio. So while the Democratic side had all the action with a staff of some seventy pages, the Republican side, my new home, had just fifteen pages total. So I assumed, then, that my nascent career as a page would be filled with a lot of bench sitting and unimportant assignments in offices which carried very little clout. But then something spectacular happened.

On October 10, 1973, Vice President Spiro Agnew resigned after having been charged with tax fraud, accepting bribes, and extortion. Two days later, on October 12, 1973, President Richard Nixon nominated Representative Gerald R. Ford of Michigan (one of our Republican members) to become vice president. I remember being surprised to find out that our own Mr. Ford, minority leader, was about to become the vice president. I also remember watching the brief announcement from the East Room of the White House on TV. Some of us gathered in the cloakroom to watch as Nixon and Ford raised hands together, and Mr. Ford accepted the nomination. The transition moved slowly for a while as the minority leadership wrestled with how to go about having our minority leader resign all his responsibilities and indeed resign from Congress. The Senate and House Majorities were also contemplating confirmation hearing dates. Hearings would begin in the Senate on the first week of November 1973.

Just about that time, on Monday, November 5, as I came to work that morning, the Head Page said he needed a volunteer to go down to Mr. Ford's office to help out with message delivery for the day. It sounded like a trap. Although I thought it might be interesting, experience told me that sitting on a couch in anyone's office for a day could be an awful assignment. Even though I had no seniority amongst the other pages, I was the first to volunteer, so I got the job. I was told to report to Mr. Ford's administrative assistant in the Minority Leader's Office. When I got there, the office was full of people running around, barking orders, and phones ringing. Mr. Ford was fully engaged in work with papers piled high on his desk as I passed by his open office door. I remember being impressed with the two Secret Service Agents who had already been assigned and were camped out in the foyer. Moments later, I was handed three envelopes for delivery to offices in the Cannon Office Building. "What do you want me to do then?" I asked. "When you finish, come right back," the Secretary said. "There will be more to do, so hurry," I was told. I went very fast and got back as soon as I could.

About 11 a.m. that morning, Mr. Ford came out of his office with about six aides in tow, and they all headed for the door to the hallway. The Secret Service guys were out front, and they all lined up into an impromptu entourage. Mr. Ford paused to introduce himself to me and shook my hand. "OK, let's go," he said, motioning to me with his head. When I asked if he meant for me to come along, he said, "Well, you're my new page, aren't you? Let's go." Somehow I had missed the concept that they didn't just want me for the day; they wanted me assigned to Mr. Ford for the next month. So there we were, pounding down the hall, a group of nine, I think. People scattered to get out of the way, and the TV cameras rolled as Mr. Ford waved and smiled. And I was right behind him. I knew at that moment that I had landed a once in a lifetime opportunity as a witness to history. I saw everything. I heard everything. Some of it good, some of it not so slick. Mostly, they were all just trying to figure it out. After all, no one had ever transitioned from minority leader to vice president before, and in the next month, until he was sworn in, Mr. Ford would have to jump through a lot of hoops. For the next thirty-one days, I would go just about everywhere he went, except for his visits to the White House. I'd like to think we became close, and I know he trusted me.

One day, toward the end of November, when the Senate was preparing to vote on confirmation, a House Republican conference was called with Mr. Ford still in charge of the proceedings. But new Floor leadership was about to be elected or appointed, and new committee assignments would be proposed. This was a big, important meeting. It was members only, so along with some of the aides, I was told to wait outside but not to go anywhere. I would be called on shortly. After about an hour, the administrative assistant burst through the door with a large pile of envelopes to be delivered immediately, all over the Capitol and House Office Buildings. One special envelope was addressed to Carl Albert, the Speaker of the House. Most of the envelopes were addressed to committee chairs and Majority Leadership, but they needed to be delivered immediately. I was told that when I got to the offices to only give the envelope to the congressman or congresswoman personally or their administrative assistant, not just the receptionist. Each envelope would have to be signed for. I was told to say that, "This envelope is for the Congressman's personal and immediate attention."

Even Carl Albert's envelope was delivered personally with a signature for the receipt. This was serious stuff, and I remember running through the halls that day, feeling very proud to be a Republican page and a part of the process. It doesn't get any better than that.

On December 6, 1973, Gerald Rudolph Ford was to be sworn in as the country's fortieth Vice President. About a week before the swearing-in ceremony, Republican pages got together and came up with the idea that we should pitch in for a congratulations gift for Mr. Ford. By now several of us had been involved in the transition in one way or another. So I was asked to find out what the new Vice President might need. I went to Mr. Ford's personal secretary to ask advice about an appropriate gift. She didn't hesitate. She said that he really needed a new briefcase. Now you need to know, Mr. Ford was in the habit of carrying his own briefcase, and even though others in the entourage, including me, would offer to carry it for him, he usually declined. And the case he carried that November was a haggard-looking piece of leather. It was old and weathered, and everybody talked about it. Some were even embarrassed. So a new briefcase it would be. I collected the funds from all fifteen of the pages and bought a beautiful new shiny leather briefcase. I think it cost about $200, which was pretty expensive in those days. So the morning after he was sworn in as vice president, all fifteen Republican pages filed into his private office to make the presentation. We were all reminded politely before entering that he was now to be addressed as Mr. Vice President even though on that day he was still in the Minority Leader's office. He accepted graciously and singled me out in appreciation, which meant a lot to me.

I returned home at the end of 1973 and found myself, now in the spring of 1974, feeling somewhat out of place in regular high school. When you've been hanging out with the future vice president and his associates, you tend to feel a bit more mature.

Vice President Ford would become President Ford on August 9, 1974, after Richard Nixon resigned. It was a weird combination of feelings. As a Democrat, I was happy to see what I viewed as Nixon's unethical behavior having consequences. As a former page to Gerald Ford, I was even more in awe. I know my friends in high school were sick of hearing about it.

Imagine, then, how much I wore my friends out when, two weeks after his assumption of the office of President of the United States, I went to my mailbox to find that week's copy of *Time* magazine. On the cover was a picture of President Ford with the title, "Ford On The Move." I was proud to see that. But after looking more closely, I noticed that, just like when he was in the House, he was carrying his own briefcase. My briefcase. The one I had picked out for him and the one to which all the Republican Pages contributed money.

What a thrill.

As a footnote, I don't think anybody in that office ever figured out that I was a Democrat.

It's a long way of saying that, being a twenty-year-old selling himself and a fledgling business to established professionals more than twice my age wasn't that intimidating. Once you've rolled with the future president, dealing with anyone else is pretty much a walk in the park.

And that's the point. Having been exposed to challenges above and beyond that of a typical high school kid prepared me for atypical performance once I got out on my own. And that's what happened to Gail, too. While I had the chance to interact with the future commander in chief of the armed forces, Gail was getting a taste of military life from a different end of the spectrum.

For Gail, being chosen to attend the American Legion Auxiliary Buckeye Girls State would change her life but more importantly mold her into the leader, business woman, and mother she would become. Girls State is an American Legion leadership program for rising seniors, teaching local and state government for future leaders.

Summers in Columbus, Ohio, are made for relaxing. With splashes of sun in the day and cool breezes in the evening, sixteen-year-old Gail Fitzgerald could have been lounging by a pool or chasing fireflies in midwestern fields. Instead, she was talking to a female West Point cadet who spoke to the Girls State attendees that year. Gail doesn't remember her name, but the impression she made changed Gail forever.

In the summer of 1976, the United States Military Academy and the other service academies finally relented to the pressure to allow females to join their ranks. In June of that year, about 125 women in classes of 1,500 each at West Point, Annapolis, and Colorado Springs began their education in the previously all-male institutions that represent the Army, Navy, and Air Force respectively. They were pioneers, and one of those brave women would speak to an audience of 1,000 seventeen-year-olds and forever change the woman that I would eventually marry.

Gail was awed by this cadet. She was poised and mature. And when Gail returned home, she decided to try and join the Long Gray Line at West Point. I'm sure she didn't know what "applying" to the US Military Academy would entail or that it would take eight months to finally get word of her acceptance—health exams, physical aptitude tests, Congressional nomination, test scores, and lots of stress and anxiety.

Lucky for me, she had already applied and been accepted at FSU because that was the family tradition. Gail was following in her mother's and grandmother's footsteps—fourth-generation Seminole. There was just a slight detour to upstate New York for thirteen weeks that would help mold her into the woman she is today.

Gail was accepted into the USMA's class of 1982, the third class with women, with a nomination from Ohio Senator Howard Metzenbaum. She reported for basic training, known as Beast Barracks, in late June 1978. The only prerequisites after being accepted were to be able to run two miles in sixteen minutes and to bring bras and underwear. In those first few years of women enrolling in the service academies, the Department of Defense was not prepared to provide undergarments for females. Everything else you could possibly need was compliments of Uncle Sam.

Gail says that by age seventeen she possessed the full complement of bras. But the two miles in under sixteen minutes was something she worked all summer to acquire. By June, her parents and brother Paul drove her to West Point to report. You sit in the bleachers of the football stadium. There's a cadet officer in dress uniform. He's a senior, and he's telling you what a great honor it is to have been appointed to West Point. You're sitting there with your parents, and then all of a sudden they go, "New cadets exit this way, parents exit that way," and that's it. There's no, "Let me help you set up your dorm room." There's no long goodbyes or anything. You can't see anybody for four weeks.

They tell the parents to stick around because at the end of the day, around 5 p.m., the new cadets are going to march out on parade in their dress uniforms and take the oath, Protect and Defend. They take you downstairs below where the football teams come out in the stadium and they say, "Drop your bags." Now, the girls, loaded for bear with the aforementioned bras and panties, are really the only ones that have bags.

Gail described many thoughts that went through her mind when she first walked away from her parents, but the most prominent she says, even forty years later, were, "Holy shit. These guys mean business."

She'd barely been in this place fifteen minutes, but already she could sense how different an experience it would be. That first day, she and her fellow cadets were issued everything they could possibly ever need. They went through a line and got bedding, toiletries, steel pots, backpacks, and even their M16s and M12s for the parade grounds.

It was like Costco but with better security. And better posture. Gail and the future troops were at attention the entire time. Even when they got to their barracks, they had to do everything in square. She couldn't walk diagonally across the hall: she had to walk across the hall and then turn. You couldn't go diagonally across the hall to get to the bathroom. She remembers walking into the bathroom with her steel pot on top of her head going, "What the fuck have I done to my life?"

She'd been there six hours.

There were two things that Gail didn't realize that first day but that would be very influential in her experience of Beast Barracks. The first was that the Senior Class each year is the officers who lead and train the new cadets during their basic training. The Senior Class in the summer of 1978, the West Point Class of 1979, was the last all-male class to graduate from West Point and they had something to prove.

The other crucial piece of information was that Gail's class was the third class in this experiment of including women in the ranks. And it was truly an experiment. Do you include the women with men? Can they tolerate the hazing and training that the men have endured for almost two centuries?

For the first integrated class entering in 1976, the men and women were separated during training, but that caused the class to be too segregated. So, the second year the men and women trained together, but the scope of the training was limited to ensure the women "could compete." That was a failure, too. It simply caused that class to be unprepared for the rigors of academy life.

So, the powers that be looked at the science of men and women. There is only one physical attribute for which men almost always outperform women, and that's upper body strength. So for Gail's class, the women trained right next to the men, step for step. The only modifications to the entire training program were that the women did the flexed arm hang instead of pull-ups, and the cocking bolt spring in their M12 parade rifle was cut two inches shorter than the men in order to execute the command "Inspection arms." That's it. Side by side, as it should be.

She had two roommates that summer. One was from Louisville, Kentucky, and one was from North Carolina. The one from North Carolina's father was in the 82nd Airborne, so she thought she was God's gift to West Point. She got in trouble a few times for fraternizing with the upper class because you're not allowed to date anybody or anything as a plebe. The other one, from Louisville, hated West Point worse than Gail did, but that was her only way to get a college education. She knew it.

Gail had options though. She had already been accepted to FSU, and so over the course of the next thirteen weeks, she weighed the harassment and verbal abuse she would receive against what she thought her life would look like in the army, or conversely if she went in another direction.

The reality was that there were no women in combat. The army officer ranks were still a big boys club. Gail had visions of a career where opportunities were available for her to rise to the top. The US Army did not promote a woman to general until 1970 and even today there are only 69 female generals out of 976 generals in the army.

Gail could handle the ten-mile runs, the target shooting, the marching, and even the severity of her all-male commanders. But what Gail couldn't handle, or didn't want to endure, was the prospect of being limited professionally. She didn't want to end up as a general's secretary. So after completing the entire Beast Barracks training program and two weeks of classes, Gail resigned from West Point.

She didn't resign because of the hazing, of which there was plenty, or because of the rigors of academy life or the five-year commitment to serve in the army after graduation. It simply came down to the fact that the army at that time didn't know what to do with a female second lieutenant from West Point.

So she made the tough decision to resign and transfer to FSU. Within a week of resigning, she was going through Sorority Rush at FSU. Although she spent that first quarter at FSU at attention (that army training lasted a long time), she flourished in her classes and as a freshman leader of her sorority. That first position was Picture Rep and lead her to me.

More importantly, her time at the Academy would impact her life, our marriage, and our business in several incredibly meaningful ways. First, when she came to Tallahassee, she was instantly more mature and responsible than any other woman.

It also taught her that no hurdle is too high, and you can really accomplish anything you truly dedicate your mind to. She had proven to herself that she could take the toughest that the leaders of the best military on the planet could dish out. And she had seen in her own physique and emotional state an ability to rise to new heights.

That confidence, toughness, and vision to see what others cannot, and take steps to make it happen, set the direction for where Bob Knight Photo would go. I still marvel at the heights we achieved as a business, and for Gail and me as a team. It's one of the reasons we are writing this book.

THREE

Pictures of History and the Business of Murder

Why Not All Photos Are Happy Memories

Afr my junior year in high school, I attended the same leadership program as Gail had in Ohio, the Florida American Legion Boys State. That session in the summer of 1974, I was elected president of the Senate and then was selected to go back to Washington to attend the American Legion Boys Nation Program. The Boys State experience would impact me for the rest of my life. I would return the following year as a counselor for Boys State and Boys Nation, and I enjoyed that so much, I pledged to go back the following year. It became something of a habit. After forty-five years, I still attend Boys State. I also had a lot of street cred with the group after being hugged by President Ford in the Rose Garden in 1975 as Boys Nation was received at the White House.

These days, I run varying parts of the weeklong experience, but my favorite is teaching the several sessions of Florida history. I put out a table on stage lined with about fifteen different historical hats and allow the kids to listen to my lectures on the rich and complex history of my home state of Florida. When I'm talking about the titans of Florida's rail, like Henry Flagler, I put on a straw hat with red-and-blue lining, like he was famous for wearing. When I talk about the role Florida played in the Civil War, I put on both a Confederate and Union soldier hat, depending on the part of the story I'm telling. I try my best to make the history of our state real and tangible to the teenagers because I myself am so enthralled with it. Partly as a result of all these years with Boys State, I've become something of a Florida history aficionado. And, I like to think, our business grew up along with the state of Florida itself. As Florida was growing like crazy with the influx of tourism, so was our business. As I'll discuss, I've had the opportunity to photograph and interact with some of the people who have shaped the history of our state and our nation. So you could say, even without a hat on, I've had an up- close view of numerous historical events.

But they haven't all been ones I like talking about.

By the winter of 1978, Gail was finishing up her senior year at Archbishop Alter High School in Dayton, Ohio, and my business was maturing nicely. My service on FSU's campus was widely known. I had every sorority house under contract to photograph all their events, and I settled into a routine of taking one or two classes per quarter (we didn't convert to the semester system until 1981) to stay in touch with school. By now I had moved from my little one-bedroom apartment on Conradi Street to a much more spacious two-bedroom apartment at Berkshire Manor, between High Road and Ocala Road. One bedroom was where the business lived, and the other bedroom actually had a bed where I slept. I had a regular cadre of part-time employees and one full-timer in the office, Marlene Pelski (later Hagen), who came to my apartment every day to run things. And my stable of well-trained photographers was growing, too. Each week, my team was covering dozens of events for my loyal customers, the fraternity and sorority members. When I wasn't on the road selling commencement services, I was spending almost every waking hour hanging out with my friends and the customers I served on Sorority Row, the houses on West Jefferson Street. I had combined my business life and my social life, forming the beginnings of the shape my eventual life would take when I became Married To It. It was a good time for a twenty-year-old to be on campus.

But all that would change on the morning of January 15, 1978, when my phone rang in the office (the other bedroom). I tried to ignore it because anyone who knew me would know exactly what I was doing at 8 a.m. on a cold Sunday morning: sleeping. There was no recorder or voicemail, so the phone rang and rang and rang. I finally got up, exasperated, went into the other room, and answered the damn thing. On the other end was an editor from the *Tallahassee Democrat*. I will never forget what he said.

"Is this Bob Knight? We understand you take lots of pictures at FSU."

"That's right," I said.

"Sororities?" he asked with a gentle tone in his voice.

"Yep," I said.

"You have pictures of the girls in Chi Omega Sorority?" he asked.

I was still waking up and was growing annoyed at the line of questioning, especially so early on a Sunday.

"Yes, thousands of party pictures going back to 1975. Why?"

"Well," he paused. "We were just wondering if you have any pictures of the victims."

Now it was my turn to pause. "Victims of what?" I asked, still not understanding but at least now completely awake and with my full attention given to the voice on the other end of the line. I knew girls at Chi Omega. Lots of them. Maybe all of them. Had something happened?

"Early this morning there was an attack at the Chi Omega house. Girls were beaten as they lay sleeping in their beds, and two of them are dead," he said. Nothing could have prepared me for that gut-wrenching punch to the stomach. My knees buckled, and he continued. "Would you be willing to provide us with some pictures of the deceased girls that we can run with our story? We'll give you photo credit."

I know that must be normal protocol for a newspaper, but in that moment, after what he had just told me, it felt like the most disgusting thing he could say. Sure, I'd do everything I could to help. But I didn't want credit for anything.

I spent the rest of the day on Sunday, and then all day Monday, in the newsroom at the *Democrat* on Magnolia Street, helping to identify pictures of Margaret Bowman and Lisa Levy at various parties and chapter events. There were dozens of each girl with their friends, their sisters, and the guys who were their guests or dates, mostly from fraternities. It was an awful experience. It made me want to quit and shut down Bob Knight Photo. I never wanted to take another picture again. I cried several times that day and so did the entire Greek community. The pictures that ran in the newspapers worldwide, and then on national and on local TV, were all taken by my team and me. They were hard for me to look at that day. They still are.

Both Margaret and Lisa were beautiful girls in literally the prime of their lives, and both were brutally beaten to death with a stick of firewood as they slept by a man whose name we would eventually all learn. They were both friends of mine whose pictures I had taken maybe thousands of times. They were both really into the party pics phenomenon, and both were hams in front of the camera. Margaret was the older and more formal of the two, always elegant and with the perfect pose. Lisa had a youthful gregariousness to her that made her the center of attention in any shot regardless of where she was standing. She would have undoubtedly grown up to be the cool mom on the block. They both lived on the second floor of the Chi Omega house, just above the front door. Whoever the killer was wouldn't have had to travel very far down the hallway. Now, because they were in the wrong beds at the wrong time, both were gone.

I felt somehow ashamed.

While I was at the *Democrat* on Sunday afternoon, I received a message through one of the reporters that Tallahassee Police detectives were on the way over and also wanted to talk to me. They asked me not to leave.

"Oh God," I thought. "Do they think I did it?"

That was not their mission, and although they did ask me where I was on Saturday night, I was relieved to find out I wasn't a suspect. They did want to know if I had seen anything. I told them I did drive down Jefferson Street on my way home from my weekly shipping at the post office. That was about midnight. There were a few people out and about, and folks spilling out of the Phyrst, the local bar which sat right next door to Chi Omega. It occurred to me later that when I drove by Chi Omega, the perpetrator, who months later we would all learn was Ted Bundy, was either getting ready to strike, attacking the girls at that moment, or had just left the house and was walking down Jefferson.

Sure, Lieutenant, I was happy to help.

They wanted much more than the *Democrat*. They wanted to see all the pictures I had taken over the past year on FSU's campus. Everything. Boxes and boxes of proof sheets for all events. I didn't mind. I was happy to help find the guy. At that point they were grasping for any possible clue as to who could have done this horrible crime. And if he was in one of my pictures, I'd want to know, too. But Ted Bundy wasn't in any of my pictures. I'm sure by the time he arrived in Tallahassee, he was avoiding all cameras. Little did we know that while in Tallahassee, Ted was living just two blocks away from Chi Omega and only one block from the Pi Beta Phi and the Zeta Tau Alpha houses.

As you might imagine, as news spread about Chi Omega, Sorority Row was in a panic. Parents of the girls from all over were on their way to pick them up and take them home but many stayed. Immediately, security was heightened. Some sororities hired armed guards, while others invited some of the fraternity guys to sleep over, which under normal circumstances was strictly forbidden. I myself slept at the Kappa Delta House on the floor of the formal living room for three nights. I don't know why. I mean what the hell was I gonna do if Ted came charging in? It didn't make any sense, but somehow it just seemed like the right thing to do.

And I wanted to be with my friends that week. Yes, I was Bob Knight, small business owner and fledgling statewide entrepreneur. But Florida State was my home. And FSU's sororities were my first clients. So an attack on them was like an attack on my own family.

No longer were the sorority houses the warm, welcoming, and charming centers of social life. The rest of that quarter, it was pretty much lockdown 24/7. There was terror in the air. All new locks on the doors were installed, and the FSU police visited every fraternity and sorority with messages of safety, including reminders that we lock ALL the doors ALL the time. The houses became fortresses, and no one was happy. There wasn't any partying going on that quarter either, although by April the annual Spring Formals returned, and we were able to get back to work on a limited basis. I think the new dresses and suits everybody wore for that occasion made us all feel better about everything.

There wouldn't really be a return of any semblance of normality on campus until Fall Rush in September of 1978. Coincidentally, that's when Gail arrived on campus, freshly delivered from West Point, New York. Although she wasn't in her uniform, she was sporting that cute, little, short haircut. And she almost always stood at attention that fall, out of habit. So the first pictures I ever shot of Gail were at that Bid Day along with the rest of her pledge class at AGD. Within a year we'd be together, and our lives would be changed forever. It's a good thing Bundy didn't attack the Alpha Gamma Delta house while Gail was there. Although, if he had, I think she would have somehow figured out a way to kick his ass.

Unfortunately, that's not the only time our work product would be required to be turned over to law enforcement officials. In 2013, with our business now national and having acquired the clientele of Santa in the malls and marathon photos, we had a team working at the Boston Marathon. As you might imagine, that meant having numerous photographers stationed at the finish line, which was where the makeshift bombs of Dzhokhar and Tamerlan Tsarnaev detonated twelve seconds and 210 yards apart. We had fifteen photographers on the course that day. Several of them were at or near the finish line, so there were plenty of images where the background might contain a glimpse of a backpack on the guys they would eventually identify as the bombers. And it would have been possible to track their movement frame by frame as runners passed by our cameras. It didn't take long for the FBI to get in touch and let us know they wanted to see all of our images.

Little did the FBI realize at first that when they asked for all the pictures they would have to review 55,000 images. But they did just that. We had to wait until they were finished before we could send the pictures to the runners. Luckily, like Ted Bundy, the bombers were ultimately apprehended. And while I was happy to assist in any law enforcement efforts, I prefer to run my photography business. The days are shorter, and the clients are much happier.

FOUR

The Most Important Client

*Winning at Business was Only Possible Because
I won at Home*

B ob Knight Photo wouldn't have grown to be the company it did if
it wasn't for our incredible staff. When I talk about being Married
To It, I don't just mean for me and Gail, though our relationship with
each other and with the company was foundational. But I think because
of our commitment level, our staff was more motivated to be "all in"
when they needed to be. We treated our staff like family. We took them
on vacations; we took them on day trips; we gave them insane amounts
of time off; we gave them raises. The joke around the office was "you can
never leave the company alive." And I'm happy to say, for many years,
hardly any of our full-time staff resigned.

The funny thing about our work family is that it varied from
my real family in one key way. Gail and I were lucky enough to have
three sons, and I love being a father to them all. But in our work family,
I had mostly daughters. We hired a lot of women and promoted a lot of
women at a time when honestly that wasn't really the norm. Even today
the company is run by our former employees who are female. Sometimes
I get asked if that was something we set out to do intentionally, and my
answer is no, it wasn't. But I do think there is a reason for it, and that

reason is Gail Knight.

It's not that Gail was a feminist crusader who set out to advocate for more females in the workplace. But as her husband and colleague, I had a front row seat to the 24/7 seminar on how amazing and productive female employees can be. If you ask anyone in the company to describe Gail, you'd get a lot of different answers, but most of them would include "bad ass."

She's Gail Knight now, but back when we met in 1979, her name was Gail Fitzgerald, a beautiful Irish Catholic girl who was in charge of delivering the checks for her Alpha Gamma Delta sorority.

You can imagine what the transition was like for Gail going from being a female cadet at West Point to enrolling at Florida State, which in the late '70s, was actually sometimes called "The Berkeley of the South."

West Point's loss was undoubtedly my gain.

It's funny to think about it now, since Gail is a CPA and financial wizard who engineered so much of our company's success, but we actually met for the first time because she had written a bad check.

In 1978 I was mainly doing party pics, and so I and my team of photographers would go to sorority or fraternity functions and take pictures of the students, then get the proofs of the pictures to the houses and allow them to order the photos, and then the money would be delivered via check. Well, for whatever reason (I still think it was an intentional way to get my attention), Gail's check from the AGD purchase fund bounced. (She insists that she knows how to balance a checkbook.) So I had to call up the sorority and talk to her about it.

Despite the accounting error, which she blamed on someone else, I could tell how dynamic and smart she was. And I was in the business of hiring smart, dynamic people. So I offered her a job.

It is, without a doubt, one of the best decisions I have ever made in my life.

Not only was she a good employee but she was an accounting major. And she was beautiful. So by 1980 we were dating. My life obviously benefited greatly because of her presence in it. But I honestly have to say, she benefited the business even more.

She worked for the company mostly as a summer job before her fall semester, but in 1981 she took Cost Accounting, which is essentially private accounting—teaching you how to figure break-even analysis, how much you make per job, and other general accounting principles. And while she didn't do that great in the class, she told me she knew enough to see that I was failing.

She said to me one day, "Bob, I don't know what you're doing, but what they teach us in this class is completely different than what you do."

Not only was she right but I was in love with her, so of course I listened. Kind of.

Business was good, in the sense that I was getting more clients. We had started to add high school graduations, and I was able to travel around and book more jobs, but my pricing was completely off. And Gail was learning enough to be able to show me where the problems were, but I was too busy chasing other business to really sit down and do anything about it. And we had other problems, too. She was about to graduate. In fact, her pending graduation is where the title of this book comes from.

In the fall of 1981, we were well in love, and she was working for me as a night supervisor. Like most college seniors, her pending graduation meant a crossroads and major decision about what to do next. She had job offers from several Big 8 accounting firms in Miami, and she was under some pressure from her parents to accept the offer and start her career.

So we were having dinner out one night, and Gail was not in a good mood. Her arms were crossed, and she was giving me one word answers. What she wanted from me about that time was a statement of commitment, as in, "Where are we headed here?"

She wanted me to be home more and be with her more frequently. Instead she was stuck, for the moment, in a revolving door of production chaos in my business, and I was often not there. I was out on the road, trying to build the business, meeting clients, and booking jobs. Compounding her frustration was her growing knowledge of the systemic problems on my back end, in terms of costs, oversight and pricing. Those were keeping the company from being as profitable as it should have been, and she knew it.

So we drifted into conversation about our future and whether I would keep operating this far-flung business that was marginally profitable, at best. It was almost to the point of her ultimatum: it's either BKP or me. But she never said that. She didn't have to.

I said, "Gail, you already know that my business is essentially equivalent to my firstborn child." She responded by saying, "No, it's more like you're married to it!" It made a profound impression.

It drove home to me this idea that I was living as a bigamist. On the one hand, I had this amazing girlfriend who made me laugh and smile and think, and who was tough and smart and sexy as hell.

On the other hand, I had this business, which brought its own sense of fulfillment. I'm a competitive guy, and winning new clients is one of the most satisfying feelings in the world. Plus, you know, it paid.

I wanted to court both wives. But Gail wasn't having it. And, at the time, I didn't think I could afford to hire her full-time. Plus, as an accounting major, Gail needed to work for two years in public accounting to get certified as a CPA. So she took the job with Peat Marwick Mitchell and moved to Miami after graduation, but we continued to date. Of course, she was in Miami and I was in Tallahassee, so we said we wouldn't be exclusive. At the time I thought it was a win-win.

I was wrong.

After she moved, my business really suffered. The Senior Class group picture market was just tanking—and I didn't have any money at all. And it wasn't just me—it was our entire industry. As the problems arose, I found myself returning to a familiar solution: Gail.

She was in Miami, but I had schools I was recruiting down there, so I could arrange it to be there on a Friday. She would get off of work from her job, and I would already be in the driveway when she pulled in. It was either romantic or pathetic.

She would usually ask me, "What are you doing here? Why aren't you working?"

I did what most boyfriends who were engaged in a long-distance relationship would do when they saw their girlfriend for the first time in a while. I handed her my briefcase. It contained all the payroll information another sorority part-timer was doing for me, plus my best efforts at something resembling financial statements and sales analysis. I wanted Gail to look at it. I wanted Gail's help. I wanted Gail—both for me and the business.

It was tough because on one hand I was selling a lot of pictures. But I was also, to quote Gail, "hemorrhaging money." And she was making $21,000 working for a Big 8 firm in Miami. But she still would look at my amateur reports.

Luckily, Candid Color was of some help. Because I was selling so many pictures, I was one of the best customers that Candid Color, our film processing vendor, had. In fact, I was their third best customer in the country. Now Gail correctly pointed out that selling a lot of pictures and making money on a lot of pictures were different things, but it was still good enough to get us a free trip to Hawaii with their other top sellers.

She may have been seeing other people, but at least my briefcase was good enough to give her an excuse to pack a bikini.

She, and her bikini, came with me, although she had to lie to her mother about where she was staying. We had an excellent time, as most people in Hawaii tend to do. And I think it solidified our relationship. Even though she was still living in Miami and working as an accountant, I knew she was the key to both my personal and financial success. By 1983, she had completed her two-year certification requirement, and our company had won another Hawaii trip with Candid Color. And this trip would be even more memorable. For several reasons.

Before we left, Gail had taken the CPA exam and was anxious to find out how she had done. She had already passed the first two sections and was awaiting word on the final portion. The morning before we were scheduled to take a sunset cruise around the cliffs of Maui, she called her roommate and said, "Open the mail."

Her roommate was a little confused, so Gail instructed her to just check the corner where it tells you if you passed or failed.

I didn't hear Gail's roommate's report, but I did hear Gail's reaction.

"Yes!" Gail screamed.

It wasn't the last time she'd say that for the day.

On the cruise, while we were anchored off the shore and watching cliff divers jump into the Pacific, I took the plunge.

With Candid Color founder Jack Counts and all his other photographer customers watching, I got down on one knee in front of Gail and asked her to marry me.

Luckily, she said yes.

The rest of the boat erupted, champagne bottles were opened, and I think just as much was sprayed on each other as consumed. As a sign of their support, my fellow passengers threw me overboard.

I don't think the cliff divers were very impressed with my form.

It was an amazing day, one that I think typified the way we would move forward, both as a business and family. And our industry colleagues, and anyone else we did business with, would be along for the

ride. We were all in, both in love and in work. We were Married To It. I
was now committed to both wives, and I knew in order to be successful,
I had to treat them both properly and help them both grow.

I'm happy to say, both worked out just fine.

FIVE

Blending

Married To It In Action

Returning from Hawaii with my most important client secured to a lifetime contract, I felt an incredible sense of momentum, both personally and professionally. Gail was such an asset to the business, and was, of course, smoking hot and brilliant, so I felt like I could literally take on the world.

In retrospect, taking on the world might have been easier than taking on her parents.

Despite my efforts to forge a solid relationship with them both, and I do think they truly respected and liked me, her parents lacked the enthusiasm for our future that the folks on the boat in Hawaii seemed to have. They were actually quite opposed.

In fact, Gail's father was furious.

"Why are you giving up this job?" Gail's father, John, demanded of her. "You don't even know where you are going to work."

My assurances that I would support her for a month or so until she could find a job on her own did little to assuage them.

Still, Gail being the headstrong woman she is, moved back to Tallahassee. Of course, I was thrilled to have the love of my life and key to growing my business by my side. But, to use a term Gail could relate to, we sort of had to fudge the numbers a bit over just *how* by my side she would be at first.

They have a joke in Gail's family: don't ever get a letter from her mother. She has three brothers, and every one of them got a letter from her mother at some point that was both searing in its conviction and deafening in its disappointment. Gail's letter arrived in her mailbox shortly before she was set to leave South Florida.

Gail's mother essentially told her that, as an emancipated, professional woman, she could do as she chose, which meant she could move to Tallahassee and even move in with me if she wanted to. But if she did choose to live with me, she would forfeit the right to have the wedding that her parents had planned to have for her.

You have to remember, this was 1983 and Gail's family was the Fitzgeralds. They were the definition of an Irish Catholic clan, with everything that entailed. Of course, Gail was outraged at the double standard of it all. She was the only girl of four kids, and still remembered the biggest argument she had ever gotten into with her parents was about how the freedoms her brothers enjoyed magically disappeared when she was a senior in high school. And like most girls, having the wedding she had dreamed of was a big deal. So she did the only thing an honest Irish Catholic girl could.

She lied.

My house at the time had an extra bedroom, and there was a phone in that bedroom that had a separate number, and the only person who had that number was Gail's mother. When that phone rang, we knew it was her mother calling, and Gail was the only one who would answer.

We called it the "bat phone."

When Gail's parents would come visit, we would take them to the apartment of one of the girls who worked for us, where Gail kept some of her clothes hanging in her closet and tell them that Gail lived there.

Gail's younger brother, Paul—who is ten years younger than she is and was still at home when we got married—told her, "You weren't fooling mom at all."

But we also weren't throwing it in her face. Like with most good Irish Catholic families, dysfunction and disobedience is OK, as long as it isn't too public.

(For the record, when he moved out, Paul also got to live with his girlfriend and have the wedding he wanted. But hey- you want to understand more about the double standards of Irish Catholic families from the last century, go read a book about the Kennedys.)

We were able to assuage Gail's parents' other concern fairly quickly as well. She was able to get a job at a small accounting firm in the same building, 306 East Park Avenue, as me. The firm was run by Ben Waddill, and I was just three offices down.

Being that close to my fiancée was terrific, but also tempting. Many times I would sneak down the hall and... ask her for accounting advice.

I'm not sure how much Gail liked that. She would always give me a hard time, teasing me about how Ben was the one who was actually paying her, and not me.

That didn't really deter me too much. But this period was foundational in our relationship, because at the time, while she had agreed to marry me, and obviously was helpful to the business, she was still determined to not have all of our eggs in one basket. So from the fall of 1983 through 1984, there she was, working as an accountant for another man but still working near me and obviously helping me at night and on the weekends.

But in the summer of 1984, something happened that made us both realize what it would really look like for us to truly be Married To It.

The 1984 Summer Olympics were hosted in Los Angeles and are perhaps best known for being the first Olympic appearance of US track star Carl Lewis, who equaled Jesse Owens by winning four gold medals that year. The Olympic games ran from late July to August 12. The AAU Junior Olympics were slated to begin the next day, on August 13, in Jacksonville, Florida, and I was confident my business's performance for that event would meet or exceed that of Carl Lewis.

Once again, my vision was on the sheer volume of it, and the amount of money we would make selling pictures to athletes and families from all over the country. Gail was focused on other aspects of it—the sheer volume of the fixed costs. With travel for our team to Jacksonville, hotel rooms, and the amount of staff we would need to shoot many events in different locations, she was skeptical that we would make enough to cover our expenses. I still remember the incredibly sweet and eloquent way she raised the point.

"How many people do you think are gonna buy this shit?" she asked.

"They'll all buy," I told her confidently. "How could you not? Parents buy a second grade picture—why not this?"

As it turns out, there are a few reasons.

One, unlike second grade teachers, who dutifully march their students to the library and have them pose nicely for the photographer before taking them back to the class, the various AAU commissioners of sports are setting out all sorts of road blocks. The swim commissioner didn't want us anywhere near the pool, for example. And the respective team coaches wouldn't get their squads together for team photos, claiming a desire to want their athletes to stay focused.

So that was our first issue—we had to work way too hard to convince coaches and managers that this was important and to secure permission and access.

Another issue is one of human psychology.

I remember a study from the University of Michigan that asked people how they liked to be photographed. The majority of respondents claimed that they liked to be caught in candid moments, for both the alleged realism it presented and the lack of hassle of having to prepare.

In reality though, people like to see themselves how they see themselves in the mirror. Posed pictures receive way more favorable reactions and as a result sell much better. And parents don't necessarily love action shots of their kids if they are making weird faces in the heat of athletic exertion. Or worse, the action photo that was of a swimmer, who was, as you would expect, under the actual water. Parents weren't all that excited about pictures of their kids' heads.

This is a lesson I learned the hard way.

The event went off just fine, and our team was out there photographing swimming, gymnastics, baseball, track and field, boxing, you name it. All told we ended up taking over 12,000 pictures, which was a phenomenal haul. I came back like a proud athlete who had just run a record time. In my mind, the hard part was done. We had 12,000 pictures. Now we just needed to mail the proofs out, collect the orders, and cash some checks!

Less enthusiastic than me, Gail was just sitting there with her arms crossed, shaking her head, because she had been seeing the money go out the door for our expenses, and she knew I had no sense of what it was costing. And she was right. I was only focused on my top line. And to be fair, we did make $100,000 in revenue for that event.

But we also had $120,000 in expenses.

This event, months before we would be married, was as significant as anything that happened to our company. Gail decided she couldn't get too far away from the numbers in the business if she was going to truly be Married To It. And I needed to be more concerned about expenses. Or at least make sure Gail was concerned about them.

So that's when Gail made the decision to quit her job and come to work for BKP full-time. I mean, what better way to ensure the financial viability of a company than to add another full-time salary, right?

Of course, we didn't tell her boss at the time. We would wait until after our honeymoon. Besides, we had a wedding to get through.

Gail was the only girl in her Irish Catholic family, so her wedding was a big deal to her, and to her mother especially. The joke was that her mother wanted a year to plan her wedding. And that's basically what happened. I proposed in July of '83 and we didn't get married until October 27, 1984. We got married in Tallahassee at the Co-Cathedral of St. Thomas Moore and had the reception at Capital City Country Club.

One thing you learn fairly early if you live in a major college town, especially in the South, is to not plan a wedding on a Saturday in the fall. We violated that rule for our nuptials, though we picked a weekend that Florida State wasn't playing. Of course, that doesn't mean the weekend worked so conveniently for everyone else.

We invited all of the people who had been with us on the boat in Hawaii when I proposed, and all of them came. (Even Jack Counts, the owner of Candid Color, who had been so instrumental in much of our success.) To this day, Jack remembers not only our wedding but the fact that he missed watching his beloved Oklahoma Sooners lose to Kansas in what would be the collegiate debut of a freshman quarterback named Troy Aikman.

But Jack is still glad he came.

We also invited everybody who worked for us at that time, and then, of course, a large contingent of Fitzgeralds from Ohio came down as well. It wasn't a small wedding, and as a typical Irish Catholic wedding, no small amount of alcohol was consumed.

But while the wedding carried on many traditions in some ways, we also started one of our own. We took a group picture at our wedding of everybody who was working for us or who had ever worked for us. Gail actually lay in the front of it on the floor with her hand at her head, and I was behind her kneeling with everybody else behind us.

Gail and I were in this moment literally Married To It, but we knew, and I think we were both wired like this, if our personal lives were going to be mixed with our professional careers, that would have ramifications for the people we worked with as well. And because I had basically been hiring my friends anyway, it wasn't hard to be intentional about treating our employees like family also. And so, Gail and I are both very proud of the fact that at every wedding after that, when colleagues and employees got married, we took the same picture. Gail even lets the bride be in the middle.

Hell, even our photographer at the wedding who took that picture was part of the extended crew. Being in the event photography business, we obviously have a lot of contacts who are capable of taking pictures. As it turned out, a guy named Bruce Heflin, who was doing the same thing in Columbus, Ohio, for Ohio State as we were in Tallahassee, offered to come down. He said, "Fly me and my girlfriend down, and I'll photograph your wedding." We said, "Sure."

His Buckeyes lost that weekend, too, dropping a tough one at Wisconsin. But his picture of Gail, me, and our team was a win. And with my wife at my side, we were now ready to go all in.

As soon as we got back from our honeymoon, Gail gave notice to Ben Waddill. And by January, she was working for the company full-time. We didn't know what her title was going to be. I already had a bookkeeper, and we had hired Gail's friend Neva Kidd, who was working as a dental hygienist and hated it, so naturally she became our Marketing Director.

That's something I've always just done—hire a person you want to work with and figure out the fit later. She didn't really have much marketing experience, but Neva was just happy she didn't have to wear floral print pants to work anymore. Win-win.

Neva had the office between Gail and me. They had been friends forever. She knew all the history and even sang at our wedding. And now, with Gail in the office full-time, she was literally stuck in the middle during our suddenly-not-infrequent disagreements.

"You can't do that," she would say.

"We are going to do it anyway," I would diplomatically suggest.

"Well, you are going to lose money on it."

"It's the cost of doing business," I'd insist.

"I guess one AAU Olympics wasn't enough for you."

Touché.

Of course, she was right. And her analysis on the AAU Olympics led to my learning to not only take a broader perspective on both the revenue and cost pieces of the equation but also yield more control of my first wife, the company, to my second, actual, human wife.

But she learned a lot from me, too.

Not too long after she had come onboard full-time, Gail had assumed control over everything inside the building, including managing all the part-time employees, while I was still in charge of all the client-facing responsibilities and field operations. Every year in mid-January, we approached the Greek organizations for reorders—taking

all the proofs and clipping them together from all the fraternity or
sorority events in the fall and letting those groups reorder, then picking
them back up and printing pictures.

Gail had ended up delivering some of the proofs to all the
houses. Well, it was early afternoon, and I told her I was going home. As
newlyweds, I was sort of hoping she would come with me.

"I can't go home," she said. "I have to deliver all these proofs."

So I asked her one question: "Do you know anything about
delegation?"

For all of her incredible strengths, she really didn't. She had
never really managed anybody. She was an accountant. And for the
business, the only people she had managed were from 5 p.m. to 1 a.m.
on the night shift, and we were just trying to get the work done. So
over the course of the next few years, as the business grew, so did her
skills as a manager and delegator. And it's a good thing, because once
we started having children, it would've been impossible for her to do it
all herself. She had to learn to delegate. Sometimes that meant having
the part-timers handle the reorders. And sometimes that meant asking
a coworker to change a diaper while she was pulling a number or a
contract for someone else.

Gail's ability to manage work-life balance as a wife, business
partner, and mother I think was truly inspiring to so many of the
women we would eventually have working for us. She adopted the
mantra "Do it, delegate it, or drop it" to help with all of her tasks, and
I think our other employees learned a lot from watching a woman
be confident enough to not only handle certain key tasks, but to also

be confident enough to not have to handle everything. It helped her, and our other team members, who then had opportunities to grow by handling the things Gail delegated.

Gail handled tasks of all kinds in our office, but she always knew who she was and her true value to the organization: she was a damn smart accountant.

She was always crunching numbers and developing metrics we could use to measure our success and profitability. There was no template, no standard accepted practice. Gail just did it.

For the grad commencement market, which was emerging as our largest though I was emotionally tied to the Greek events, the biggest metric was dollars per graduate photographed.

She was also figuring out how to improve our processes, which could best be described at that time as unwieldy.

Picture this: you mail out all these proofs, and all these orders come in without much specific language, and you have to sort them. They come in with a proof card and a check. Everything was by check. You have to keep the proof cards and sort them by school, because when you send the orders into the lab you have to put the proof cards in roll and frame order. Then you send the stack of cards overnight to Candid Color, and they print based on the card, which contains the images sequenced by roll and frame number. Our staff would then have to look and say, *OK, that is roll 10, frame 7, print roll 10, frame 7, etc.* It was very manual.

As the guy making the sales, I wasn't too worried about it. We just did it because that's how we had always done it, all the way back to the late nights in my apartment on campus.

But Gail was determined to figure out a better way to do it. And like a lot of Gail's best ideas, it involved a trip to the liquor store.

She went to the store and got the discarded boxes for cases of 16–20 ounce Budweiser beer bottles. We called them Bud boxes.

We had 300 schools at the time and needed to have nineteen actual cases. On each bin of the case we put a label for every school, and then stacked them up on the wall of our office. So, thanks to Gail, we invented an inexpensive way to sort the orders from each school. We didn't need to drink the beer either. I hate Budweiser.

But it was free. And it worked.

Every school had a bin in a Bud box. The orders were processed in the bookkeeping department because that's where the deposits were made. Gail was making sure we had proper internal controls. All I wanted was the money in the bank as quickly as possible. So Gail's intrepid crew of accounting majors hired from FSU reviewed each order, separated the checks from the proof cards and filed each card into the correct Bud bin. The deposits were prepared and taken to the bank every day. With the proof cards from each school sorted in the Bud boxes it was easy to manually add up the sales for each ceremony. Our software system didn't have this sophistication until 1992.

Not all of Gail's innovations involved beer boxes.

Gail figured out that you could save money by buying in bulk and by sorting outgoing mail by the first three digits of the ZIP codes. So she made a wall of cubicles, and we started sorting the mail ourselves. It may seem like a small thing, but it allowed us to get our costs down, which when you consider the volume of prints we were handling for the universities and high schools, who came from ZIP codes all over the state, it was a massive thing.

Gail was incredibly hands on. She was always more in the office than me, and while I was meeting with principals and clients, Gail was making sure we didn't go bankrupt. She was also a perfectionist. Probably a trait of her profession. If a mother of a graduate called to say that we sent the wrong proof, that meant we had identified at least some of the graduates from that ceremony incorrectly. Most of the time, it's an easy fix. But sometimes, correcting the sequence of a graduation ceremony can be like a jigsaw puzzle. And Gail loves a good puzzle. She would review all the proofs and figure out the correct sequence. It was tedious, tiring work, and she did it all the time.

If you talk to any of our employees from back then, they'll tell you to a person that Gail was a role model. Because while she was incredibly smart and hardworking, she had no ego and would do any job that needed doing. And it helped with morale. If the owner isn't above doing a task, then the employees sure as heck couldn't think they were either.

This was so important, because during grad season, when we have tens of thousands of proofs to identify and orders to sort, you have to have an all hands-on deck mentality. You're going to do whatever it takes to get it done. You're going to do the mailing to get the film processed, you're going to stay up, get to the airport, have it shipped to Oklahoma City, whatever it takes. She was never afraid of any job and was willing to do anything.

In the spring of 1990, we had just moved into our new house in northeast Tallahassee, and one May weekend I was down in Orlando, managing Grad Night at Walt Disney World®. FSU's graduation was that Saturday morning, and another massive client of ours, Mosely High School, had their prom in Panama City that night. Gail, as a hands-on, do whatever it takes owner, had some equipment in her car that needed to get to the FSU shoot, and I couldn't be there to help.

Fun fact about Tallahassee: it actually receives more annual rainfall than Seattle. Quite a bit more.

Second fun fact: with all the trees, power goes out during rainstorms quite often.

So it was on this fine morning that, as Gail was headed to FSU's graduation, the power was out, and for some reason, she wasn't tall enough to pull the rope to lift the bottom of the garage door open.

She has many talents, but power lifting isn't one of them.

Undeterred, she went over and introduced herself to our new neighbors at 6 a.m. by pounding on their door and asking him to come open the garage door. He complied, and she was able to get out, make it to the graduation at FSU, and then drive to Panama City. Gail and the team shot the prom, and by the time they got back to Tallahassee, it was 3 a.m. Sunday morning, with the film from both events due to be shipped to Oklahoma City from the Tallahassee airport at 6 a.m.

Our office at the time was much closer to the airport than our home was, so Gail, ever mindful of the math and metrics, deduced she could sleep more on the couch in our office than if she had to drive to our bed. She did, got up and took the box to the airport, and then came home and slept until 2 o'clock in the afternoon, with her first task on Sunday afternoon being to get up and take a bottle of champagne over to our neighbor.

That's Gail. And that's what having no ego, a ton of work ethic, and a willingness to do whatever it takes to get the job done looks like.

The best part? I was oblivious to all of it. My role as the CEO meant I was protecting values and adding clients. That weekend I was working Disney® events, but I was often out of the office, taking care of other clients, or meeting people I hoped would become clients. And frankly, that balance worked perfectly.

Gail would tell me that if I spent too much time in the office, I ended up just making everyone crazy.

"We just want to do our jobs," she'd tell me. "We just want to get our work done. Don't you have some place you need to go?"

Of course, the place I went was to our house. Where Gail still had to deal with me.

SIX

Stealing from a Mouse

Bringing the Magic Home

One of the best compliments I've ever received from my employees came from Michelle Jagers, a long-time employee of the firm and close friend of our family, when she said that I was a good listener. "I've never met anyone who is a good manager," she told me, "who talks more than they listen."

Obviously, if you're going into sales, or plan on having any sort of success in a customer service enterprise, you've got to be able to listen. Listening is how you accumulate information, how you learn what the customer wants, what they need, what they're afraid of, and what they're proud of. It's all about the exchange of information that you can use at some point down the road to your advantage. But listening, as any preschool student worth their salt can tell you, is only one of the five senses. You can also learn and steal information by watching. And, while I hesitate to tell you this because of what I've already disclosed about my ability to trespass at graduation ceremonies, in the interest of full transparency, I will disclose the following: I have stolen a ton of shit.

In the summer of 1985, Gail and I were still in our first year of marriage, and we were given an opportunity to attend a trade show in

Dallas as representatives from Candid Color. Our network with Jack Counts and Candid Color had been valuable in many ways up to that point already, but we had no idea when we signed up to present for the National Association of Secondary School Principals just how much more valuable that network was about to become. Even though the association was for school administrators, it included many more people and contacts than just administrators: everyone who does business with the principals or their schools, and anyone who *wants* to do business with the schools. So when we signed up, we might have been placed next to the people trying to introduce chocolate milk into the lunchrooms for all we knew. But that's not what happened.

We went to the trade show to try to pitch graduation pictures not only for our business in Florida but also for Candid Color's other customers from around the country. We were just trying to sell the concept. Today, the idea of graduation photos is hardly new. In fact, with the advent of smart phones, you could argue it's even passé. In 1985, however, the concept of these graduation pictures was relatively new. It had been around for about eight years, and even then only adopted by fewer than half the schools in the country. That's why we were there—to meet school administrators and convince them that, well, gee, wouldn't their school's kids and parents be so much happier if someone was there to capture the moment of their graduation and offer pictures of that special moment in a few small, affordable packages at no cost to the school or obligation to order.

The booth right next to us at the trade show was sponsored by the Magic Kingdom™ at Walt Disney World, who had reps trying to market Grad Night, their special offering of access to the park for high school seniors over late night hours each May.

So over the course of the three-day convention, while Gail and I were hawking our graduation photos to any and all comers, we would engage in some idle chatter with the Disney reps, talk shop, and swap stories about the joys and challenges of working with high school students. We might have even shared a meal together if I remember correctly. And over the course of the three days, they were asking us questions I thought were just routine and polite (the Disney people were very polite) about our systems, how did we keep track of the proofs and prints, how quickly did we deliver them, and I in turn asked what I'm sure I thought were relevant professional questions like, "How hot does it get in the mouse suit?"

Then at the end of the show, Kitty Phillips from Disney gave me her card and said, "We need to have a meeting."

We did not realize it, but they'd been checking us out during that period of three days, asking us questions because they knew we were from Florida. Suddenly I was thankful for our decision ahead of the conference to dress up in suits—which was not typical of all attendees. Now everyone dresses business casual at those types of shows, but back then we wanted to be upscale. After all, I was only twenty-eight-years-old and looking for any way to stand out and look credible amongst my much older peers. Plus, the rule was always to dress better than the president or the principal.

So when they asked us for the meeting, we were both kind of blown away, both with excitement over the potential of what working with Disney could look like and also just the idea of working *with* Disney.

It's important to remember that the Walt Disney Company of 1985 wasn't the multinational conglomerate that owned ESPN or Star Wars. In fact, Disney was just a year removed from a lengthy *New York Times* profile in which the future of the empire was very much in doubt. Disney had just hired Michael Eisner to come in and be CEO in an effort to turn things around, and he was bringing in a guy named Jeffrey Katzenberg, who later forged the key relationship with Pixar, to run their movie studio. The *Times* article pointed to the next two years, meaning 1984–85 as being a time frame that would "represent the first time when all the pieces that they have been assembling over the last several years become fully functional. If they end up justifying the investment, Disney is going to have a tremendous surge in profitability. Otherwise, people may be looking for an angel to come in and buy it. "

As it turned out, Disney would be just fine. And we were lucky enough to go along for the ride.

Even though we were newlyweds without children, we were, like most Florida residents in the 1980s, big Disney fans. Before I had proposed to Gail and she was living in Miami for the year and a half, we would meet in Orlando for the weekend and go to the Magic Kingdom and the newly opened Epcot Center™, where you could "Drink around the world." I think it's fair to say we were considered global elite by the Epcot staff. The only thing missing about Disney from our perspective was a casino. If they'd have had one, they'd have gotten even more of our money.

The point is—we loved going to Disney.

So when Kitty Phillips asked to set up a meeting, I headed down there as fast as I could. Kitty explained that they had these hard ticket events. When the regular park is closed, it is opened up for special events and they offer pictures for all of these events, such as for Mickey's Very Merry Christmas Party™ or Grad Night. They needed someone to take pictures there, which Disney provided to the guests as part of the entire experience package.

They had been doing it for years by handing out a square 3 x 3 image from a Kodak instant camera. Kodak had developed an instant camera like a Polaroid, but it had a crank on the side of it. The problem was that it was a little too much like Polaroid, and so Kodak had to stop selling and using the cameras because Polaroid won a patent infringement suit. Without Kodak's Polaroid patent pirate, Disney didn't have a way to have their untrained cast members take pictures. But they wanted to keep providing photos for their guests, so they went to Kissimmee (just southeast from the parks and actually closer to the Disney parks than downtown Orlando) and hired a local photographer to bring a crew out and shoot the event.

I don't know if you've ever been to Kissimmee, but in the mid '80s Kissimmee was a much more rural Central Florida town than major entertainment capital, and the photographer and his crew embodied as much. I don't mean this as a slight to the restaurant, but the local crew had about as much corporate polish as a Waffle House waitress. But at least the waitress will get your order right—the Kissimmee crew, not so much.

The local photographer messed it up all kinds of ways: bad pictures, sloppy records, slow or nonexistent deliveries, but the reason he was fired was because he and his team would not dress right. They would not adhere to the Disney look, meaning clean-cut, no facial hair, no jeans—business attire. Even worse, Disney officials caught one of the photographers smoking on the stage. The Guest Relations Manager said, "You can't do that."

These days, things have evolved, and smoking can not only be banned by some employers but also by most private businesses and even some cities. But in the 1980s, smoking was still fairly commonplace in the workplace, especially for freelance photographers. But Disney was insistent about no smoking from its workers. There was a big lawsuit about it, and Disney actually prevailed because they argued that everyone working there wasn't really an employee: they were "cast members." They claimed that everyone there was just playing a role, and that Shakespeare had been right when he said, "All the world's a stage."

In the Magic Kingdom, that was absolutely the case.

The employees were all actors, and the stage was called the Magic Kingdom, and there was no smoking on stage. This made an impact on me—and fundamentally changed how we prepped and dressed our own employees in the future.

The Magic Kingdom General Manager explained what they wanted done, which was essentially taking pictures at a designated area and coordinating the delivery of the photographs in a timely manner. I may not have thought about the benefits of a potential partnership for the three days we were working side by side in Dallas, but as I listened to this Disney rep, Kitty Phillips detail how she wanted our company to do the thing we'd literally been doing better than anyone in the state, I realized this was right up our alley.

I knew then that they didn't care about the pictures. They just presumed we could take the pictures, and they were right. What they wanted was a good performance. Once I got my hands around that idea, I gathered the people I knew would do a good job with it, and our first event was Mickey's Very Merry Christmas Party, and then the Cast Christmas party in 1985, but the big event was going to be—if we did that correctly—Grad Night the next May.

After the meeting, as I was walking back to my car, I took a moment to pause and look around at my surroundings. As I scanned the vast expanse of the world-famous Magic Kingdom and thought about what our partnership could mean, I had no doubt we would knock it out of the proverbial park. But we would have to change a couple things.

Gail and I realized, partly after hearing about the Kissimmee photographer, that we needed to not only meet but exceed their expectations of what their photographer cast members would look like. Remember, our entire ethos about sales and service meant giving the customer exactly what they wanted. In this case, what they wanted wasn't free prints; it was corporate-looking photographers who would blend in with the Magic Kingdom experience.

No problem.

But meeting their expectations meant we needed to change our culture a little bit. Before, I would allow our crew to go in coats and ties to major events, but if Disney wanted us in suits, you better believe we were going to wear suits. I told my photographers I would loan them the $200 to go buy a suit, but they had to get one.

"I'm just a photographer," some of them said.

"That may be," I responded. "But you aren't going to be a photographer at Disney World® without a suit."

Some of them still pushed back. The part-time photographer community was a distinct one. And of all the words you might use to describe it, "corporate" wouldn't have been on the list.

"If you don't want to do this," I countered, "then this might not be the best job for you."

That ended the conversation fairly quickly.

Women had to step it up, too—they needed to wear hose, which wasn't ideal for either the May heat or the December chill. But Gail and I actually got less pushback from the women than we did our male photographers. Women, I guess, don't need as much pressure to dress up.

When it came time for our Disney debut, I had us ready to go and literally dressed to the nines. Disney had us enter through the back door, so we would stage in the Contemporary Resort hotel parking lot and take a shuttle bus they provided over to Tomorrowland and then all walk in through the entrance as one team. There were about thirty-five of us, and getting off the bus and then walking in, we looked like Wall Street lawyers coming in—guys all in suits, women in hose and dresses. I don't want to overstate it, but we looked slick, man. And the best part— Disney just ate it up. Once they saw what our team looked like, I think they were sold. They didn't have any idea what the pictures even looked like, since they only saw them if someone wanted to complain about them. The pictures went to the customers directly. But seeing us "look" the part was enough, even though the pictures were the best they ever had.

In fact, we looked so much like part of the Disney World team that 95 percent of the guests assumed we were actually Disney cast members. They'd routinely come up to us and ask us about events going on, when was Justin Bieber going to be on the Mainstage, where were the bathrooms, etc.

No problem. I made sure all of our staff knew the park from front to back and knew who was playing and when.

That's how we kept the contract for fifteen years.

This upped our game. It changed our business. It made us a better company. Our standards had to increase, and I could blame it on them (Disney). As we said, our rule was "I want you to be dressed as nice as the person on that stage, and if that is the president, I want you to look like the president. I want you to dress in the same way that he is." It just became the standard that if you were working for us, you were in a business suit. Not a coat and tie, but a suit: a shirt and a tie and dress shoes that are shined for men.

I realized, thanks to Disney, that our photographers were also just playing a role. Yes, they needed to be able to point a camera and shoot the shot, but from a business development perspective, just like when I had my guys doing party pics at sorority and fraternity functions, the technical ability was much less important than the role they played and the look they brought to the role.

We didn't just steal from Disney's look though. Negotiating the deal with Disney was a learning experience for Gail and me. Gail was a CPA, and she took our cost management very seriously, or at least as seriously as she could with someone like me running around and setting things on fire. But Disney showed us how to take things to an even higher level from a cost management perspective.

The first December we were there, Gail put together the numbers and told them we would need to do their events for $1.40 a picture, which Disney would be paying us. So the first time we did that, we did it for that price. Then the next time we went back, they asked if we could do it for less money. Gail said, "We can't." For some reason, they didn't take us at our word.

So Gail went down there and showed them all the numbers for what we were spending per print. Their commitment to creative problem solving when it came to saving money was impressive. I mean, you think about this giant company, but they are sweating things down to the fractions of a cent. Literally.

They asked questions like, "Where do you get your film? Can you buy it from us?" They were looking at every line that we had. We got it down—we were to the one-hundredth of a cent. Of course, we were selling them 380,000 prints a year at all the events. We got the price down to $1.325 by letting Disney print the address cards that went with the picture in the envelope. They could do it a lot cheaper. We kept the same margin and Disney saved $20,000. Everyone was happy— including the actual recipients of the photographs.

Everyone that came into the park was eligible to get a free picture. On Grad Night, for instance, for five nights we photographed every single person who was there. About 14,000 a night—70,000 pictures. We were contracted to deliver the pictures in five days, but we usually delivered the pictures within three days, and with each picture we sent out we included a card in case they wanted more pictures. The way we got away with that was we said to Disney, "What do you want us to do if they want more? This is a customer satisfaction issue here, and we are happy to figure out how to do that, and we think it is probably a good idea and will make you look good too."

"Yeah, do that," the Magic Kingdom's Vice President ordered.

Don't have to tell us twice.

We didn't make a lot on the reorders, but it was a nice enhancement to the service for the guests.

It cost the kids sixty dollars to go to Grad Night, but for us it was a $500,000 contract per year. There were three events: Cast Christmas, Mickey's Very Merry Christmas, and Grad Night. More importantly, it was only three checks. It was the Cast check, a Mickey's Very Merry check, and a Grad Night check. Three checks, so it wasn't any of this processing of every single order from every single graduate and his grandma in Jacksonville and his aunt in Georgia, and here is a five-dollar order and here is eight-dollar order. They were, for that and other reasons, our favorite client, even though the margins were not as high. But the volume was incredible. And it was a half million dollars over twenty nights a year. Eventually we expanded our services into three more parks—Mother's Day at Epcot, special parties in the MGM

Studios, and finally Disneyland® in Anaheim, California.

But we benefited just as much culturally as we did financially.

We talked all the time about the Disney look and the Disney values. Several members of my team went down to Disney University for Disney 101, which is the Disney orientation, which was very helpful, too. There are lessons there that transfer well to any business. They had to learn about the history of Disney. The only thing that was less relevant to Bob Knight Photo was that our employees who went to the Disney orientation also had to memorize the Seven Dwarfs.

We ended up keeping that contract for fifteen years, thanks in large part to Gail's father. Again, Gail and I were Married To It—the business and our family. And that meant in-laws. And while some men may not have wanted to take advice from their fathers-in-law, I respected the man. I mean, he raised his daughter to be part of the third female class in West Point history, become a CPA for a major firm, and have excellent taste in men. What was I going to do?

"Bobby, you need to make sure there is an option in there," Gail's dad, John, would say. "Do they really want to rebid this thing?"

So, in the original contract, at John's suggestion, we gave Disney an option to renew every year for the same price. And every year, for fifteen years in a row, they did.

Finally, they took the service in-house, but not before we made nearly $8 million from the partnership.

We improved our image and look at every event we went to, whether it was for Disney, a high school, college, mall, or marathon. And Gail got even more detail-oriented after seeing how Disney could scrutinize even the smallest of factors.

But Gail and I always loved that we got to keep working in the Magic Kingdom in part because of the wisdom of Gail's dad, who himself was part of the Small World of Bob Knight Photo.

SEVEN

Focus

Making and Keeping Customers For Life

I f I am going to be remembered for anything from my career, it will
probably be the time I dressed up in drag at the Candid Color
awards ceremony. But while "Bobette" may be remembered for her
shapely calves and willingness to go all-in for the good of the evening,
what I'd like to be remembered for, and the thing I'm truly passionate
about, is our emphasis on customer service and the lengths we would go
to maintain those relationships. Almost as far as "Bobette."

At the start of my career, when I was driving all over the state
and trying to build my business one conversation and relationship at
a time, I would listen to a lot of books in the car. One of my favorite
authors in those years was Tom Peters, who was really big in the '70s and
'80s as a business author. He wrote several books, including *In Search
of Excellence*, which was about best business practices. Then he wrote
Passion for Excellence, which is about the best CEOs and what they do
to first obtain, then ultimately maintain, that status.

One of the things he said in *In Search of Excellence* really hit
home for me: profit isn't everything. As counterintuitive as it may seem,
Peters' point was that you don't always have to look at the bottom line

if you're trying to look at a company over a period of years. If you focus too much on the bottom line, you could drive the company downward.

For his book, he interviewed a number of CEOs, and he quoted one of them on the topic. "Profit is like health. You need it, and the more the better. But it's not why you exist."

That really resonated with me, because I knew in the long run if I provided good service, I would make a profit. And providing good service may actually include not making as much money as possible in some interactions. Some of my competitors never understood this concept when we would compare notes on our philosophies and practices. But early on, thanks in part to Peters' writing, I developed this idea that **sales and service are inseparable.** To sell a customer was to service a customer. And whatever service you needed to provide, that's what the cost of doing business was. Because, as Tom Peters emphasized, it quickly adds up. You realize that this is not a customer that this year will generate a couple hundred thousand dollars in revenue and make a margin of maybe $50,000 a year. Over the course of our relationship, if it lasts twenty years, *this is a million-dollar customer*. If he wants an additional president's album, I'm going to do it for him. I'm going to make him indebted to me. Along those lines, another book that I enjoyed was by a car dealer in Texas named Carl Sewell. He wrote a book called *Customers for Life*. His whole goal was to make sure that he did such a good job that people, once they did business with him, would refuse to go anyplace else. Thus, they became customers for life, both in his Service Department and his dealership.

So I'm driving around the state and thinking about these

concepts, making sales and service inseparable, and creating customers for life. And it worked. Clients generally responded positively to me, but more importantly, our service was exceptional. Not just in terms of showing up and shooting events, but in dealing with the customers over the phone and on site. We had essentially two main categories of customers: the schools for which we were providing the service of shooting their graduations, and the parents and families of the students who would be graduating. The parents paid us, but the schools and their administrators were the reason we got in the door. So while my job was to communicate and connect with the school administrators, if my staff wasn't taking care of the actual paying clients on the back end, I would hear about it on the front end. This dynamic, and the balancing of the responsibilities as a leader, made me appreciate another of Tom Peters' points—the role of a successful CEO.

In the early '80s, with business being somewhat flat, I was heavily in the trenches. I would do everything from making contacts with the schools, organizing the teams, and shooting the actual ceremonies to working with the staff to make sure the film was developed and sent to the clients. Eventually, thanks in large part to Gail, we became more systematized, and as a result we saw the business grow, both in terms of the revenue and the staff we would need to manage the projects.

Suddenly, being a good networker and photographer wasn't good enough anymore. My role changed. I had to become a good manager and get out of the trenches. Eventually, I even put the camera down altogether. This wasn't that easy for a guy who got his start having co-eds scream my name as I wandered around sorority and fraternity parties. But Tom Peters had good counsel on this, and it helped me get over my own personal habits and focus on what the organization of Bob Knight Photo needed.

Tom Peters said that the only job that a CEO has is to communicate the goals and protect the values of the organization. The best CEOs don't do anything. They stay way out in front, and point directions, and communicate the goals, and protect the values we felt were foundational. For us, that meant establishing service as a competitive advantage. We were going to out service everybody, and we were going to create customers for life. So that's what I was trying to do—make sure our employees understood that, no matter the issue, we, as a company, were committed to exceptional service, and I'm trying to make customers for life.

That means, and this would happen all the time, if a competitor came in and wanted to do business with a school, the school wouldn't even entertain the idea of talking to anybody else. That's what we were trying to do. So I would be looking for opportunities to give stuff away. If someone said, "Gosh, we're having our 100th anniversary of our university, and we're going to have this little celebration. Can you help us with that?" I would fall all over myself to help them with that. When they said, "Well, how much would it cost?" I always answered, "It's our pleasure to do this as a thank-you for your business."

And it didn't matter who it was. I remember one time an employee named Fernann Yozviak came into my office and said, "Lake Gibson High School in Polk County is having a golf tournament.

Debbie Donahay, our contact, is on the phone, and she wants to know if you'll sponsor a hole."

So she's standing in my doorway, and I toss my head to one side, and I just stare at her. She goes, "Oh yeah, OK. I'm sorry. Yeah, OK. I got it." That's how I knew I was doing my job the way a successful CEO should. The values I was projecting and protecting were trickling down. We still sponsor that golf tournament more than twenty years later.

Pretty much everybody in my organization got it. It's going to cost me maybe $500 altogether—a photographer for the better part of the day, an album or two, and a hundred 8 x 10s. Then, of course, I would personally deliver it. For $500, you can't buy that kind of loyalty.

Ironically, the person I had the hardest time instilling the values of the company into was Gail. But not because she didn't understand the value of it. Unlike me, she was concerned about the logistics of it.

Ever the accountant, she wanted to know how to track the costs of these additional services we were providing. "Where do we code this? Do we code this as part of the commencement?"

Of course, that was the last thing on my mind. But that's why we made such a good team. She realized the wisdom of it, but she wanted to account for it, and she wanted to make sure it didn't get out of control completely. So for our internal accounting, she created new categories to track these services so it wouldn't influence the accounting for the performance of the events. That had to stay intact. We weren't just doing this haphazardly, but I was literally giving stuff away as often as I could. And I was encouraging our staff to do the same. We were doing it everywhere we possibly could.

One day, I got a call from a gentleman named Mark Rosenberg, who was familiar with us because of our work with Florida International University's graduations. He started as a professor at FIU and then worked his way up the academic hierarchy, becoming a dean and provost for FIU, and then Governor Jeb Bush named him as the chancellor for the Board of Governors for the entire State University System of Florida.

Having known him from FIU, I had kind of followed his career at FIU, and he had followed mine. He knew I was in Tallahassee, and so as Chancellor of the State University System, he had offices in the Turlington Department of Education building which was in Tallahassee as well. That office, as it turned out, lacked something the head of all the Florida universities thought it should have.

"Do you have any pictures of the state universities?" Dr. Rosenberg asked me. "Do you have any iconic pictures of the campuses and stuff?" he said, "Because we don't have any pictures of our universities in our office."

I don't know if it would be humanly possible to say, "Absolutely" any faster than I did. A donation to the State University System would be on the way shortly.

He just wanted a few pictures. He would figure out what to do with them. Of course, I went way overboard and framed 16 x 20s of all, at the time, nine universities and delivered them. Of course, they were all signed Bob Knight Photo. We even sent somebody over to help hang them.

Like I said, way overboard.

For her part, Gail only wanted to know how much it was costing. And she thought it was too much, pointing out that the free pictures would have been sufficient, and that he certainly wasn't expecting a professional photo hanger. But that was exactly the point. And I'm convinced it is what Tom Peters would have done.

Of course, Rosenberg would leave his job as Chancellor of the State University System and become president of FIU. He became the perfect example of customer for life. I didn't deal directly with Dr. Rosenberg when he became the president, but I was confident that if a question came up about service or anything related to our contract, that I would have every opportunity to fix the issue and keep the business.

Even though they weren't our main point of contact, I still made it a point to make sure that I knew all of the university presidents and that they knew me. Every graduation ceremony, I'd go back to what's called the robing room and shake hands with them, introduce myself, or reintroduce myself, and say, "I just wanted to present myself and say that we're happy to be here. I took the liberty of making a mark on the stage where you're going to stand to shake hands. If there's anything else I can do for you, if there's any other extra pictures you might need, please don't hesitate to let me know."

None of them ever asked me for anything like Rosenberg did, but I still sought out opportunities to cultivate relationships with them when the opportunity arose. I even employed a university president's son for a while who was living in Miami at the time. He said, "You know, my son might be interested in taking pictures." I said, "Oh, really?" Within a couple of weeks, he was on my payroll, and he was good at it.

The point is that I had a very early education on the power of service and trying to establish customers for life. And it worked. People don't believe me, and in fact the consultants who were auditing our business before one of our mergers definitely didn't believe me, but we almost never lost any grad customers. Like ever. In fact, if we ever stopped working with a school it was usually because we fired them for being too small or too difficult to work with.

Now, every once in a while, we would lose a school to the yearbook photographer. After all, the yearbook photographer was usually somebody who was in the school every day. But they didn't specialize in commencements like we did. So my stance on yearbook photographers was to convince schools to let them do everything else, but when it comes to commencement, whoa boy, you'd better be using us because they don't know what they're doing. And we could prove it. But every once in a while, we'd lose one to them, probably a dozen altogether over forty years.

Now, in the incredibly rare instances that we did lose someone, or we had a complaint, I tried to instill in our staff what an opportunity it was for customer recovery. Recovery is a great opportunity to solidify your relationship. I mean, mistakes are going to happen. Things are going to get crushed in shipping, a name is going to be wrong, or truthfully maybe the picture just isn't that flattering.

Not everyone is a runway model, you know.

But you can't be perfect all the time. So when there was an opportunity to recover, we'd be all over it. Failure is an opportunity to

improve further. We actually had that written on a wall somewhere.
I remember Anne Munson had a plaque on her desk that used to say,
"If you don't take care of your customers, somebody else will," which
was a nice refresher to remember. If we got a call from a client that was
a complaint, we would do several things. We would, first of all, send
flowers. Then I'd write a letter and send it to multiple people at the
same school, saying what we've done about it. We would aggressively
apologize and say how we've corrected it.

Quick example—we would take these Senior Class group
pictures, a service we provided for about 130 schools throughout
Florida. You remember the Senior Class pictures. Usually in the
gymnasium, folks lined up on the bleachers, and the appeal of it is that
it's everyone in your class in one photo. (At least that's supposed to be
the appeal. Honestly, they weren't big sellers because they were kind
of expensive, and there's not a tremendous amount of detail, and the
parents don't really care who else is in the class—they care about their
sons or daughters and sending portraits to their relatives. But it became
a tradition, and the schools liked the pictures, so we took the pictures.)

Well, remember what I just said about there not being that
much detail in the Senior Class pictures? Every once in a while,
somebody would flip the finger in the picture. Now normally, we would
get rid of it. Before digital, in a film environment, we would just take
it out with a touch up, usually with a sharpie marker. We would just
draw little dots over that finger so that you couldn't see it. In a digital
environment, of course, it's much easier to Photoshop over those
juvenile acts of societal rebellion.

But every once in a while, some bozo in the back row would discretely have his little finger out there, and we'd miss it. So that was one of the complaints that I got one day. This assistant principal called me, and she was, I think the technical term would be, all over my ass for allowing him to have his finger in the picture and me not fix it. On paper, it's not a big deal. But it sure was to her.

Unfortunately, at this point all the prints had been delivered. But that didn't matter to her. She wanted to know what I was going to do about it.

"Well, what would you like me to do about it?" I said.

"I want you to reprint all the pictures," she said.

"OK. Absolutely. We will reprint all the pictures. We'll get right on that today. You should expect them back by Thursday. We'll roll them up and redeliver them all."

She was flabbergasted. She said, "Well, I don't know that you need to go through all that."

But I insisted. "Well, that's what we're going to do," I said. It meant we weren't going to make any money on that event that year, but I didn't give a shit about making money on a Senior Class group. They had a really good commencement. So even though we made a mistake, do you think she's going to go to a competitor next year?

She's not going anywhere.

This, too, was a value I had to project and protect. I had seen author Steve Mulvaney's list of the steps to sales recovery. We would have our people follow those steps exactly. All our Client Service reps, including me, and our entire Customer Service Department had these little reminders of how to recover on our desks, which we could refer to any time we had a recovery opportunity on the phone.

First of all, listen without interrupting. If the customer is calling to complain, they're mad and they need to get it all out. You must make sure that you hear them. So don't interrupt them. Let them finish and just listen to what they're saying.

Then thank them. "I sure am glad you called and told me about this. If you hadn't called, I would not have known. So I appreciate you giving me the opportunity to fix it."

And it needs to be a sincere thank-you. Because, really, they are doing you a favor. If you're having a problem in one area with this customer, you almost certainly are having one with another. Maybe many others. Complaints are the engine light coming on in your car. They are opportunities to prevent much worse damage from occurring.

Number three is apologize. Again—sincerely. "We're so sorry. Here you are trying to do business with us, and we made this mistake."

That leads nicely into asking what we can do to fix it. Whatever comes out of their mouth, we do that. For customer service, it's usually something like, "Well, reprint my order." Well, that's easy. It doesn't cost very much. With parents, it's not even about their business. I'll reprint a hundred parents' orders if needed. What I don't want, and what I did everything in my power to avoid, is them calling the school. So I'm going to be all over this recovery because I'm going to do everything I can to save the school. And I made damn sure my team knew to do the same. Who cares if I don't make money on that particular order? I mean, I usually still did make money off it. But I was willing to lose money.

I find that many sales-oriented people and businesses have failed to learn the lesson of Tom Peters. They are too focused on profit, and as a result, they end up not making as much of it as they should.

When our company was bought out by a private equity firm, Gail and I stayed on as employees, but weren't running the show anymore. And I saw firsthand what a different approach looked like. For them, it was all about the bottom line. So when I wanted to give away pictures or give away services to our best customers, they would say, "No, no, no. You can't give away ten 8 x 10s to this customer. It just costs us too much."

Well, that's ridiculous. They cost like a dollar a print. They had completely turned my business model on its head. They didn't give anything away for free and stopped assuming that the customer was always right.

In the short term, their profits may end up increasing. But I promise it will ultimately impact the overall health of the company.

EIGHT

Depth of Field

You're Only as Good as Your Weakest Employee

I don't want to sound like I was giving away everything for free with no recourse or accountability. I had the world's best accountability partner—Gail. Whenever I was giving something away, Gail was there, writing it down, because while it may be true that too much focus on profit can negatively impact a business's health, someone still needs to measure blood pressure and cholesterol on occasion. That was Dr. Gail.

Gail was instrumental with measuring metrics. For graduations, we determined that every metric had to be measured based on how many people crossed the stage. If a student crossed the stage, then that is an opportunity, so they counted in the number. We looked at the average order by school which was based on how much money we took in and how many people ordered. Based on that, Gail was also able to calculate percent ordering, so we knew how many people we photographed that actually ordered. The metrics we monitored were average order, percent ordering, and dollars per graduate. But the one we watched the most was dollars per graduate. Total amount of money deposited per school divided by the number of people who crossed the stage, not just the number who we were able to market to. We were pretty good, but back then even the process of taking the pictures was laborious.

We were still having to switch out cameras and physical film. So you would shoot a whole roll (with thirty-four images), then quickly switch it out for the next camera. And on the busy days you had a loader, which was another person to load and unload the camera, then hand it back, loaded, to the photographer. The graduation ceremony does not slow to meet the photographer's pace. If a step is missed, or the film is not loaded or not handed off correctly, then that is a graduate who was not photographed. That is a big deal. Back in the early days, Gail loaded film for me at a few graduations. We would use two cameras and a backup. Her job was to hand me the one that was loaded and ready to shoot and take the one that I was using and unload it. The first time we worked together, she had never loaded film before, and our first exchange of cameras was a disaster. She misloaded the film, and it wasn't advancing, and the rewind knob had come off in her hand. I turned around to look for the new camera, and she was just gesturing and pointing at the camera. I just had to pick up the backup to keep going. She finally figured it all out.

Eventually, we realized that the person who was loading the camera was a critical position. Some of our competitors would just hire people out of the audience. And, for the most part, those unsuspecting aunts or cousins, who were there to watch a relative walk across the stage, did not know what they were doing. It was very risky.

So in an effort to not have to hire complete strangers, we tried to have two photographers on the team whenever possible, and they would just switch positions at the end of each roll. But on the busiest days, we weren't able to do that. So as a last resort, we came up with SWIL, an acronym for "Shoot While I Load." So we would occasionally find someone who was support staff with the event, or a member of our team who wasn't a photographer per se, to help out for a few frames. It is really easy to show someone what a picture is supposed to look like because you are standing in the same spot, and the graduates are crossing in the same line. So the stand-in photographers operating as a SWIL would shoot the first four or five frames. When it's time to switch cameras, the SWIL simply steps up in the exact spot where the photographer was standing and starts to shoot. It was all handheld, no tripod. This way the photographer, the professional, loads the film, gets the next camera ready to go, and switches out with the SWIL. This dance is done at the end of each roll for the entire ceremony. The SWIL never reloads since getting the film advancing in the camera is much more important than the potential of four or five slightly uncentered photos. It was one of our staff who came up with that idea. We got some really good people to work for us early on who had some really good ideas. Our motto was to just hire good people—we didn't care what they did before—if they could speak, and they looked like they were intelligent, we considered them as a possibility.

This was one thing Gail and I agreed on. For example, we hired the bartender from Carrabba's, Natalie Madden. We loved the bar at Carrabba's, and we knew her from hanging out there. Every time we left there, Gail and I would say, "She is really smart. We should hire her." She was going through school, earned a finance degree, and she even got another job, but then eventually she came to work for us, and now she is Vice President of Finance for Iconic Group. She has worked for us for almost ten years. We were always looking for good people. Always.

We were always recruiting on the local college campuses—FSU, FAMU, UCF, FIU, and TCC, but mostly FSU. We specifically recruited through a lot of sororities. We would hire for the spring grad season, and they would know that the job was over at the end of the summer, but there were always a few who rose to the top. We knew we had to figure out a way to keep these standout part-time employees around. We had some part-time positions through the regular school year. Working for us in the summer was a great summer job, and it was finite. They were paid well and could work as many hours as they wanted, and when they were done they would go back to school for the fall. Working for us worked with their school schedules. But some people would rise to the top. Gail and I talked about it. It was different in all areas—Customer Service, Production, and Operations—but we knew we had to find a way to keep them around, so we would just ask them if they wanted to stay on and work part-time during the school year. And many of them would stay. Then we would try to keep them on even after they graduated. Often, our best part-timers would become full-timers.

And we didn't just hire help for the offices.

Our twins were born in February 1996. The following December was one of our busiest months because we had the Very Merry Christmas Party at Disney and all the December graduations. And now we also had twin boys, plus our oldest son Timmy who was just a few years their senior. Gail hired Matt and Joanna Tamplin, a young local couple that babysat for us once in a while, to actually move into our house. Timmy was five and the twins were eight months old, and the Tamplins lived with us that December because Gail needed help. I was traveling all over the state, working these big events, and Gail was working lots of hours, so she just paid them to live at the house and help out. She was resourceful. Gail did not have a model of the working mother. Her mother perhaps did not really understand, but she still helped out. When our first son was born, her mother was keeping him at her grandmother's house near the Myers Park neighborhood. Gail was going back and forth from shoots at the Civic Center to her grandmother's house to nurse Timmy. Her mother thought Gail had lost her mind. I think Gail may have agreed.

Her mother questioned Gail that day. She asked her, "What is your focus?" Meaning, I suppose, that her focus should be solely on her son. He was two weeks old.

"Mom, this is my life. All of it," Gail told her.

Gail's parents helped a lot with Timmy, but when the twins came along it was too much for them to keep all three. It was also hard because Gail felt like they were questioning her too much. She felt like she had to answer to her parents again. So she promoted our housekeeper, Barbara Long to nanny. She still works for us today. Gail realized that it was worth it to spend the money to have the kids taken care of without any judgment. Barbara does a great job, and she loves our kids. Gail knows how to hire good people. And God knows she needed to. We used to say we don't have plants in our home. We don't because you have to be able to scream or talk to get noticed. If you can't make sounds and speak, you're not going to get the attention you deserve. That's where Barbara, as our housekeeper, nanny, and personal confidant, came in. She paid attention to the things that didn't scream loud enough to get Gail's or my attention. And she may have even watered the plants.

It truly took a team to keep all the members of our household alive. Because while Gail and I loved being parents, we also loved our business. And we were trying to get it to grow up along with our sons.

NINE

Damien Lamont Byrd

Our Team Gets the Point Guard We Didn't Know We Needed

Because we were a relatively small team of full-time employees, Gail and I could be particularly choosey about who we hired. Very few people were hired at BKP without going through the interview process, where I was always the second interview. If you couldn't get past me and my impromptu "sales tests," you weren't getting hired, regardless of what other connection you may have had in the building.

One exception was Damien Byrd. On a Monday in January of 1996, I was sitting at my desk, planning the rest of my week. We had just completed our weekly Monday meeting. Our receptionist, Virginia Sawyer buzzed me. "There's a very nice young man here who wants to see you", she said. Now Virginia and I knew each other well enough, that I knew if she said, "nice young man" and "wants to see me" in the same sentence, it was code for, "You need to meet this guy". So, I said, "Send him up". Before I could hang up the phone, he was already up the stairs and standing outside my open door.

"I hope you remember me", he said. "I'm Damien Byrd." It took

me a second, but then I remembered well. I first met Damien when
he was 17 years old as a rising senior at Port St. Joe High School, a
small public school in Franklin County, which is about an hour south
of Tallahassee. We first met at Florida American Legion Boys State in
Tallahassee, the same youth leadership program that Gail and I both
attended between our junior and senior year of high school. Then
in 1993, as now, I was a counselor for the program, and I remember
Damian as a rather brash extrovert who exuded self-confidence. He ran
for state office and lost. But his campaign gave him plenty of time on
stage and I remember thinking, "Hey, this guy's a pretty good speaker
and seems very mature for his age". I would find out later that he was
also a pretty good athlete. He was captain of the PSJ High Basketball
Team. When I asked him what position he played, he said point guard.
That figures, I thought. He was actually the lightening quick, trash
talking, cocky point guard, who was always in trouble with the referees.
That's my kind of guy and someone I'd like to have on MY team.

So, at Boys States' conclusion on Friday night, I pulled him
aside. I asked him where he intended to go to college, he said he wanted
to go to Florida A & M University. Since FAMU is in Tallahassee,
I knew he'd be coming back in a year. So, I told him (somewhat in
passing), "If you ever need a job while you're in school, come see me."
And that was it. I wasn't even sure he knew my name or how to find me.
I'm not even sure he knew what business I was in or whether I worked
for the State. I've told kids that before and since, but the follow-up is
mostly non-existent. I never expected to see Damien again.

So here we are, 2 ½ years later, he's in the second semester of his sophomore year at FAMU and out of the clear blue, here's Damien standing in my office. We had only moved into our new building, named the Gail F. Knight Building on Commonwealth Ln, a few months before. So, I was immediately impressed that he found me.

"It's so nice to see you again, Damien. Have a seat." I welcomed.

I sat on the edge of my desk and he sat right in front of me in the guest chair.

"Now, what can I do for you?" I said slowly.

He leaned in hard and with all seriousness he said, and here's the punch line,

"Mr. Knight, I'm here to collect my new job. You said come see you, so here I am."

I had to laugh. Where do you go with that? He comes in here and pretty much demands I give him a job.

What balls.

We chatted for a while to get reacquainted and before long I realized he was actually interviewing me and asking dozens of questions. It occurred to me that when he walked in, he had no idea what we did as a company. But he didn't seem to care. I said, "What do you know about photography." He replied, "I think I'm good at it. I take pictures all the time." We both knew that wasn't true. Turns out, he didn't even own his own camera.

Backed into a corner with nowhere to turn, I finally said, "OK Damien, you've got a job. We'll start training you this week, but we really won't be busy until the spring." With that, I called down stairs to the Director of Operations, who was at the time, Paul Fitzgerald, my brother in-law.

"Paul can you come up here for a minute."

"I will be right there." he said.

"Paul, I'd like you to meet your new photographer, Damien."

Paul was confused at first. He cocked his head, squinted his eyes and stared at me for a minute. He knew that he did the hiring in his own department. He knew the protocol for the interview process, and he knew we never hired photographers in January. While other departments were busy in the winter, he knew that time of year was the least busy for his department and the part-time photography crew. But he also knew I wasn't crazy, and I must have something in mind. He never questioned my directive. I asked Paul to get him up to speed as soon as possible and show him around and get his papers signed. As he and Damien left, I've never seen a kid more excited. I could tell he realized his gamble had paid off. I could tell that he'd be a hard worker, dedicated and appreciative for the chance. Exactly what I was looking for.

By the time May 1996 rolled around Damien was well trained, although inexperienced. He soaked up tips from the veterans and little by little, over the course of the rest of 1996, became one of our most capable photographers and sought-after partners in the field. He was so proud to be a professional photographer. When he told his mother what he was doing for work, she couldn't believe it. Being a professional photographer was a pretty big deal in his community. It instantly raised his image in Port St. Joe.

Damien was described by a friend from FAMU as "Dapper". He was that. He spoke well and was comfortable in any setting of colleagues or high-ranking clients. Always impeccably dressed and immaculate in detail, we could send him into any challenging setting, and he'd come back with rave reviews, quality images and his paperwork in perfect order. Then, along with Sandi Donlevy, he became our unofficial social chairman, planning parties and outings for the staff to enjoy. Whether it was an impromptu happy hour, or a company bowling tournament, Damien and Sandi were out front in organizing our events.

When he graduated from FAMU in the spring of '98, I knew I had to keep Damien in the organization as a full-time associate. But I didn't have a job for him at that point. It didn't matter. We needed the bench strength and the diversity. Gail and I would put him in management training and when a position opened up as regional manager either in Florida or California, he'd be first in line. At this point in his nascent career (he was only 22, I think), he would have to go through an interview process and consider his options before making what I was hoping would be a long-term commitment. I asked him why he wanted to stay on at BKP in a bigger role. He said, "Because I know that you and Gail will give me opportunities." That was all I needed to hear.

He had an impressive career which spanned 18 years, as a Regional Field Manager and ended up as the firm's Quality Control Manager, one of the top slots in the corporation. More importantly, he was a mentor to many new employees over the years. He trained dozens of young photographers, including my son Tim who actually started taking commencement pictures while he was in high school. They were regular partners on the road and traveled all around Florida and the

SE United States. Together they built a reputation known for their consistency, with few or no screw-ups and nothing overlooked. Later when Tim was in college, he was invited to return in the spring to shoot all over the country. Even though Tim was busy, he found time. But he said he'd only work another season if he could work with Damien.

For me, Damien was more than a friend and colleague. He taught me a lot. We worked together in the field many, many times, mostly when he was the Team Captain and I was working for him. I loved to watch his silky performance in the field, making it all look effortless, even though it wasn't easy.

Running a commencement ceremony for us meant being able to not only manage the team of photographers, but work with commencement coordinators on staging and commencement choreography or adjusting the position of the podium or a potted plant. Damien could finesse prominent people with a smile on his face and a mission on his mind. Damien had high ranking officials with numerous degrees doing the things he needed, to do his job correctly and thinking it was their idea.

But of course, Damien could handle operating in these self-important stratospheres. He had been doing it his entire life.

Damien was my window into the world of what it was like to be a professional black man in a mostly white dominated society. Everywhere he went circumstances were just a little more different for him. Sometimes people would be rude if not downright abusive. Damien took it all in stride. He persevered his way through the difficult moments of his career. He never complained.

It bothered ME royally, because I was the one who put him in those difficult circumstances, like working for a particular all-white fraternity or a "good ole boy" high school administration in Alabama. Even security sometimes would treat him differently. If we entered a commencement venue together, even though we were both wearing suits with nametags and carrying our equipment, sometimes I would breeze through the entrance, while Damien had to stop and show his ID. Damn, that would piss me off. I hated the way some people would treat this elegant gentleman. If I were to say something to the Security Guard, like "he's with me", that only made it worse. Damien didn't like it. It only made him feel like he couldn't get it done on his own, even though he was the most capable member of the team. But it wasn't his fault.

Everyone who knew Damien has a favorite story about him. Some are charming and funny about some antic he pulled which made everybody laugh. Some stories are about his heroic work habits, including all-nighters with no sleep, to get images and materials back to the office on time. And sadly, some stories are about situations he had to endure to get his job done and the barriers thrown up by a few misguided overly cautious white people who just thought they were doing their job, but instead just made his life more difficult. But he pushed through anyway.

So here is my most favorite story of Damien's perseverance:

First a little background as a reference point.

Throughout the history of our firm, indeed all commencement photography, the primary Achilles heel to performing in the field has been battery power for our flash units. You remember in pervious chapters, I discuss the need for our flashes or strobes to be able to recycle very quickly, so that the strobes can fire ever second or two. We were constantly in pursuit of the best strobe/battery solution. We tried all the models of all the brands; mostly Metz, Sunpak and Vivitar. Each brand of strobe required a different design and power of battery. And there were different materials used in each unique battery. Some were powered by lead acid batteries (like a car battery and really heavy). Eventually a lithium battery became popular. But in the late '90s and early 2000s we were using Sunpak strobes with Nickel Cadmium batteries, or NiCads for short. But the Nicads which came from the manufacturer weren't big enough to go the distance and might run out of power in the middle of the ceremony. So just like in 1976 when we first started, we needed to reengineer the strobe/battery configuration. We started using a bigger, off-the-shelf NiCad, normally used for miniature race cars. But that battery was about 4.5 inches in length and 2.5 inches wide. It weighed a full half pound. You put a few of those together and you've got a full shotput. They also had to be mounted on the back of the strobe, not inserted inside the strobe as the smaller NiCads did. No one told me that to be a commercial photographer I also had to understand electrical engineering.

      The next hurdle was figuring out how to efficiently charge these much larger batteries. At night, while on the road, we would take all our batteries and chargers, to the tune of 15 to 20 pounds with chargers and find enough plugs in the hotel room to plug them all in. Every few hours you'd have to get up and rotate the batteries. Then we started using multi-receptacle power strips, which helped but was not the final solution.

Then in 2001, Rick Chartrand invented something which would revolutionize battery charging for us. He took an old Halliburton photo case, the size of a large briefcase, then wired in two power strips in the case and made it so that you could get to your room and plug in the whole case with one plug coming out of the case. Eight batteries could be charged at the same time. It was beautiful and eventually we made dozens of them and gave each team a battery charging case.

Rick named the contraption "Set it and forget it", as in set it and go get a full night's sleep. Its nickname was the acronym of the primary words. So, it became SIFI and labeled as such. The only down side was that a random lay person looking at it, couldn't figure exactly what it was or what its purpose was. Picture it. It's a bunch of wires, all squeezed together or coiled and connected to something blinking. It also got hot after hours of usage and much of it was wrapped in black electrical tape. That's right. When you first opened the case, it looked like an Afghani incendiary explosive device.

More than one of our team Captains had been stopped by TSA at an airport to explain what it was. Frank Mix was detained at Seattle's Airport until the authorities were convinced enough to know it wasn't dangerous. I think they called the bomb unit, but by the time they got there, Frank had been cleared.

OK, back to Damien and his nightmare Saga. Fast forward to Grad season 2011. By now we had acquired over a dozen other photography firms and had a national footprint. We had a total of 12 regions nationwide. Damien's region was the entire southeast US. But he was so well respected, that he was often requested to help out in other regions on busy weekends. Not all regions were busy at the same time.

So, Doug Wyland, by now regional manager for the Southwest, requested that if Damien was available, he fly to Tucson to help out with the Univ. of Arizona commencements which sprawled a full weekend and several venues. He was assigned to be team captain at the Tucson Convention Center. He flew into Tucson in the evening without incident, rented a car and spent the night at the Doubletree on Broadway. His arrive time at the TCC would be 10:00 am the next morning.

The next morning, Damien got up, put his suit on, shined his shoes and was poised to leave the hotel at about 9:30 am. While he was brushing his teeth, there is a knock at the door. It was Housekeeping asking if she could begin to clean the room. He said she was welcome to start now; he was just leaving. Here is the first glitch. Damien had plugged in his SIFI and it had been charging batteries all night, the case was open, and the maid saw it, blinking lights and all. Apparently she was panicked and ran out of the room immediately. Damien couldn't figure out where she had gone in such a hurry. Her cart was still outside, but she was not in the hallway. He gathered his things, got in his car and headed for the Convention Center. In the meantime, the housekeeper was trying to find the General Manager. By now Damien was long gone. In her thick accent, she told her boss that there was a suspicious black man on the 3rd floor. He had a silver case "with a bomb in it."

You can imagine the calamity which ensued. Police were called
to the hotel. They searched his room. Registration information was
recorded. The name of his firm was noted which implicated both Doug
and me. The cops called the office and said they were looking for a black
man named Byrd carrying a silver case. They wanted to know where he
was going. Someone explained to the officers that his name was Damien
Byrd and he was headed for the Tucson Convention Center for today's
commencements. Keep in mind, on this day, the TCC would be filled
with over 15,000 people. Given the facts at the time, the Tucson Police
Department incorrectly assumed that Damien was a Terrorist, probably
from the Middle East or Africa whose intent was to blow up the Civic
Center. So, eight officers descended upon the Civic Center with lights
and sirens. They found Doug Wyland and the stage set-up guy. There
was a sense of urgency. "We're looking for a black man with a silver case,"
one officer said. Doug replied, "Well you must mean Damien Byrd,
one of our photographers." He confirmed that's who they were looking
for. Doug then said, "Well the silver case is right over there, under that
folding table. But Damien's not here right now, he's in the robing room
with the platform party and taking pictures." This news didn't seem to
give the police much comfort. So, four of the officers sprinted for the
hallway to look for Damien while the other 4 circled the silver SIFI case,
not daring to touch it.

Damien was unaware of any of this of course, so he was
surprised when he was grabbed by both arms and taken away as if he
were a serial killer. The University President and his guests weren't told

anything at that point either and were left to imagine what the amiable Damien could have possibly done to deserve the harsh treatment. It certainly didn't help his reputation or the credibility of the firm. Damien was finally ordered to open the case, while some of the officers took a step back.

Eventually they all realized it wasn't a bomb, but as more officers arrived, they were so invested in the threat that Damien was detained (not arrested) and grilled for over an hour. He was jacked-up as they went through his pockets and called the FBI to see if they could help with a background check. They eventually released him, and he actually went back to work for the next ceremony. I'm not sure I could have handled it as well as he did. Damien would say later back in Tallahassee, "Yea, it was just another day at the office for me," as his co-workers laughed it off. I knew better. Doug told me later that Damien was clearly shaken by the incident, especially since he was the last to know what was going on.

But that was Damien. His mantra was keep your head down and plow through the adversity. He didn't deserve all that, but I admired the way in which he handled it. It wasn't the first time or the last time, that he'd have to talk his way out of a dangerous situation. When I finally got the chance to talk to him the day after the incident, all I could say was, "Damien, I'm sorry. I am so, so sorry that this happened to you. Can you forgive me?" Ironically, he had to calm me down and talk me off the ledge. There were tears all around.

Tragically, that wouldn't be the only time we shed tears for Damien.

On Dec.18, 2014, Damien, then 38, died unexpectantly and shockingly, from complications related to a heart condition he'd had since birth. He kept it to himself, but apparently knew that he had a congenital abnormality in one of his heart valves which would, or at least could, cause him to pass at a relatively early age. Damien had a twin sister, Dia who had the same condition and, tragically, had passed away nearly two decades earlier.

I didn't think about it at the time, but I realized later that she must have passed around the same time Damien had come to our office, ready to claim "his" job.

Gail and I were about to go see our son Tommy act in a play when we found out about Damien's death. We were at dinner in Thomasville, Georgia when Paul Fitzgerald, my brother in law who first trained Damien how to be a photographer, called us with the news. Apparently, Damien had started experiencing chest pains, and in typical fashion, tried to handle it himself. He drove himself to the hospital while, as best we can tell, he was having a heart attack.

Even the brightest stars can't shine forever.

We still went to the play, but all I could think about was Damien. Seeing my biological son on stage only reinforced my bond with this cocky point guard from the rural panhandle who talked his way into my office, his job, and our lives. The play was a Christmas Carol by Dickens, but Gail and I couldn't concentrate on the performance.

The next few days were really, really hard. Our whole world was darker. Without Damien's light, how could it not be?

We rented a bus to take everyone who wanted to go to Port St. Joe for the viewing, funeral and reception. We emptied a good chunk of the building, and co-workers came from all over the country.

That was Dec. 23, 2014, two days before Christmas. It rained all day.

In some ways, it hasn't stopped.

Damien's energy is still shining through. While working with us over the years, Damien built his own family. He left behind a beautiful wife, Lysheenya Phillips Byrd, son, Daylin Lee Byrd and daughter Devena Lori Byrd.

As part of the grieving process, I took solace in the way Damien's loss was felt throughout our corporate family. I realized that, at about the time he lost his sister, he became part of the Bob Knight Photo family. He worked for Gail and me his entire professional life: we were essentially the only job he ever had. In his death, I knew we had to honor the impact he had on our lives.

We knew we wanted to do something to help Damien's children. I'm proud to say that every one of our full-time employees donated money towards a trust that we set up for their education. For all he had given Gail and me, it was the least we could do. Who knows what Dailyn and Devena will grow up to be, and what they'll do professionally? But damn, I know who they came from. And we were honored to help make sure Damien's legacy will live on through them.

For Gail and me, Damien represents the very best of what we want our legacy to be. We didn't just hire people, we adopted family. Being Married to It means sharing your lives with the people you work with and sharing your work with the people in your lives. We hired the person, not the position. So, we didn't hire people we thought were right for the job. We hired people we thought were right for our lives.

TEN

Making Money While Wandering Around

Because You Can't Lead Your Team From Behind Your Desk

O ne thing Gail and I believed firmly in was that if we were truly Married To It, then that meant our employees were our family. And while it may be taboo in some families, in our company, we talked about everything. Especially money.

In the late 1980s, Gail established a monitoring system to let all the full-timers know how we were doing. We shared all our numbers with the staff—revenue, costs, basically everything but the salaries of their coworkers, or Gail's and mine. But everything else was open. It helped everyone, regardless of their position, feel like a key member of the team. We reviewed them monthly, and told everyone that, if we did well, they were a key reason why. And if our numbers were less positive, we were counting on them to help us get those numbers up. Plus, we stressed that it was all confidential, and I think they liked knowing they were on the inside of something.

Gail would put up these little charts that would have indicators of how we were doing on a daily basis, including our dollars per student, average order, and sell through rate. The weird thing about our

business was that it was done on speculation—meaning we invested
our resources on the front end and were just hoping the money would
come in afterward to justify our expenses on photography teams and
marketing for the schools we were servicing. So almost on a daily basis,
people could understand, based on the sales that came in, how we were
doing. That created a lot of buzz, because if we were doing great, people
were talking about it.

I would come back from being on the road and the staff would
greet me with a, "Hey, Bob, did you see the numbers? They're looking
really good." At some intervals, the staff knew more than I did because
they got the information before I did, because I was out of the office. I
think that was very powerful for people to feel like they were included.

If we weren't doing so well, then that was OK, too. And that
happened, especially in early May of some years. Early May was peak
season for graduation shoots, and it was the first time our investments
could be measured for their returns.

We're kind of out on a limb the first week of May because we
have spent a lot of money to get ready for the season, so we're banking
on May to be a really good month. So if the first week of May doesn't
look so good, it would be easy to...I think the technical term is freak
out. We did our fair share of that, mostly because of timing. Depending
on when we measured, it might have looked like our early May numbers
weren't as good as last year, but that could have been because the
calendar varied each year. If a big school or several schools moved back
a week from one year to the next, the effect would, at first glance, be
substantial. But that didn't keep us from panicking. It was ok to worry

about it, because it kept everyone motivated. That was big because back then a lot of our sales would come in on the phone. So we had an opportunity to improve our sales if we did a good job on the phone. I liked hearing our staff, if the numbers weren't looking so hot, go get after it on the phones.

Because they knew that when we did well, we made sure everyone benefited.

We had a significant bonus program that made sure that if Gail and I were making money, so were they. That was huge for morale and also helped to thin the herd, because everybody knew that if one employee is messing up, let's call him "John," then he's affecting not only the company but also their own bonuses. That helped our internal controls in several ways.

First of all, the staff would be all over John to go fix himself, improve his performance, and if they could, they'd offer to help him to improve. But then, every once in a while, the mainstream staff would push somebody out. Michelle would come into my office and say, "So-and-so is an idiot."

I'd usually respond with something like, "Tell me how you really feel, Michelle. What's going on?"

"Well, these things are not getting done. At the first opportunity, we need to replace him," she would say. And I knew she was speaking on behalf of the staff at large.

Gail would know before me, because they'd all go to Gail first. And it was challenging for me, but no matter how much I liked the person, if they said, "This is not getting done, and it's affecting your bonus, and it's affecting my bonus," then I've got to make some changes. And we usually did.

That's one benefit of having an empowered staff. And we only wanted to enable that sense of empowerment. Gail would put on little classes about finding inefficiencies and opportunities for revenue enhancement. We were sharing our numbers with them after all. So we might as well teach them some basic accounting as well. And Gail was an excellent teacher.

You have to remember that when Gail and I were in our thirties and forties, we were still hiring people in their twenties. Our staff was always really young and still had what we now would call a "growth mindset." They weren't set in their ways and were ready to learn—especially if it meant making more money. That's one reason I would pick youth and enthusiasm over experience anytime—because we could teach them.

I wanted motivated young people who were enthusiastic and would be impressive to an older person like an assistant principal, or a principal, or a college president. I can dress them up in a suit and, even though they only look twenty-two, they're going to act a lot older. But that also meant that, when it came to finance and accounting, most of those people didn't have a clue. And they weren't the only ones in the office that needed to learn.

You have to remember that I wasn't an accountant. I was a communications major. I never even took any business courses except marketing. So while Gail was teaching our staff, she was teaching me, too. There was a time when I didn't know anything about accounting, but she would constantly spend time with me, sit me down, and show me. Now I'm really good. I mean, I can look at a balance sheet, and I can look at a profit and loss statement and understand it. That might sound like a weird thing for a grown man business owner to brag about, but it represents the impact Gail has had on me.

Now I can look at not only my business but the financial statements of the organizations I've served on the Board of Directors for as well. I've been able to help them look at a profit and loss statement and understand what the hell is going on. I can now tell if there are systemic financial problems. Gail taught me how.

So while I was teaching Gail about service and the value of spending a little extra money to get customers for life, she was teaching me the numbers. That was a really good partnership. I taught her service ethics, and she taught me accounting and finance and helped me understand how to treat people.

But I didn't just learn from Gail.

As I mentioned previously, I learned a lot from some of the authors whose books I would listen to while I was driving around the state, meeting with clients and growing the business. One of the most valuable lessons I learned was from author Tom Peters, in his book *A Passion for Excellence*. Peters taught the concept of Managing By Wandering Around, or MBWA. It is simple enough, but for me it would become a powerful management tool. Also encouraged by author Steve Mulvaney, the idea was to get out of my office on a regular basis and walk around. I wasn't looking to see if someone was slacking off. I was learning and letting the staff know that I understood what they were doing and appreciated the effort. Peters said that when a CEO is down on the plant floor, he sees the processes better, and studies showed that it also made the CEO look smarter and more engaged in his own firm. Now on any given work day from 1985–2006, my office employed twenty-five to thirty associates, twelve to thirteen full-timers and about eighteen to twenty part-timers. That made the full-timers the managers, with each having a corral of part-timers to do the work of his or her department, be it Production, Finance, Customer Service, Shipping, Equipment Management, or Client Services. During commencement season, April to July, that number in the office could balloon up to as many as 200 part-timers, with hundreds more photographers in the field, who rarely came to the office.

So as often as I could, usually about twice a week, I would schedule time to get out of my chair, wander around the office and say "Hi" to everyone and listen. I wanted to be sure they all knew who I was and that I knew them. Hardly a week went by when we didn't have someone new in the office. Remembering their names was a big deal, and I was often told how much they appreciated that. But my real purpose was to look for opportunities to compliment them and their work. And I tried to be as specific as possible. Like, "I just heard part of your conversation with that client, and I thought you were excellent. I noticed how you blah, blah, blah....... Nice job. Well done." And I'd say that loud enough so that everyone around could hear me.

My purpose was to catch staff members doing SOMETHING RIGHT. My purpose was to positively reinforce the behavior so they would do it again next time. My purpose was to help build their self-confidence. I would never try to correct them during MBWA. That might come later in a conversation with their manager, one of the full-timers, but never on the floor and never in front of other co-workers.

One other aspect of MBWA was it gave me the opportunity to write notes or cards to individuals with whom I was impressed. Sometimes, for no particular reason, I would ask an associate or two to come into my office so that I could give them a compliment. If their manager was available at that moment, I'd ask them to join us. Well, the first result was that it created chatter in that department. Co-workers would say things like, "What did he want? Did he yell at you? Are you in trouble? Then they became shocked to find out I just brought them in to say thank-you. Before long, being invited to my office was worn like a badge of honor, and the star performers had more pep in their step. Most importantly, with confidence, they always repeated the positive effort we were looking for.

I also used MBWA in field operations. Training photographers to be good event managers was paramount to our success. Training season in April and May became an exercise in teaching photographers how to take the pictures over and over again without making mistakes, having a back-up plan, and understanding how to get out of a jam, since the ceremony could not be paused. But we spent much more time, weeks in some cases, teaching event management to the young photographers. That part of the training was about everything except firing the cameras. And for good reason. If the team lost control of the event they were working, then it didn't matter what the pictures looked like because there would probably be no pictures or sequence, making our service worthless. So our teams had to constantly anticipate problems as the ceremony progressed. We did indeed have to improvise, adapt to changing circumstances, and overcome the obstacles.

MBWA in the field was much more difficult than in the office. First, because when things went wrong in the field, most or all of our systems could come crashing down. Second, everything that potentially could go wrong was all happening at the same time, so team captains had to see everything at once, constantly scanning the entire room and the stage. All of our photographs were carefully choreographed or posed, even though we were taking pictures in three different places at a rate of one frame every 1.5 seconds. Thirdly, every ceremony is unique. Even though some were similar to each other, every school was different.

So in the 1990s, when we were servicing more than 600 ceremonies annually, my job as president shifted from Top 5 photographer in the firm to putting down the camera and trying to visit as many ceremonies as I could, even though, on any given day, there would be multiple ceremonies at the same time in different cities. When I was assigned a role on the team for a particular venue, I most often focused exclusively on event management and never picked up the camera. But I'm a bit of a control freak (go figure), so I saw my job as that of making sure nothing in the entire building was going to happen without my knowing about it.

For several years in a row, toward the end of our season, we would send a staff of about forty-five to fifty photographers and crew to photograph the Miami-Dade and Broward High School graduation ceremonies. It was a five-day marathon of a week. We assigned a full

team to each venue, and they would camp out there and shoot as
many as three ceremonies each day. In Dade County alone there were
six venues: two arenas, two performing arts theaters, one gigantic
gymnasium, and the Miami Beach Convention Center which resembled
a large air plane hangar. Each venue came with its own set of obstacles
and challenges for the team. After the assignments were made, I took it
upon myself to visit as many ceremonies as I could, wandering around
each venue at least twice each day, talking to school administrators,
giving positive reinforcement to the photographers, and checking
the stage setup. Sometimes I'd bring lunch for the team or some extra
needed equipment or film. By this time of year, all the team captains
were seasoned veterans. My role here was that of facilitator. I became a
resource for them if something was needed, or if I needed to graciously
ask the Superintendent to hit his mark while passing out diplomas.

That is how I got so good at slipping in the back door or stage
door in the middle of the ceremony. In this role of going from one venue
to the next, my first obstacle was always the guy protecting the stage
door from people who weren't authorized to enter the back door. Now
you have to remember that I would often show up late, after "Pomp and
Circumstance" or even during the speeches. It was unusual for anyone
to enter the stage door after the beginning of the ceremony. After all,
anyone important enough to enter the back door was already inside. But
keep in mind that before the ceremony there was a parade of folks going
through that door. There was the school administration, several teachers
assigned various roles to play, the School Board, my photographers
who arrived early in the morning, and even the school band, each with

a music stand. So even though I showed up with a suit and my name tag, and even though I was absolutely authorized to be there and could prove it, there was always some skepticism about my intentions. After all, the ceremony started forty-five minutes ago, and I wasn't on the list of the platform party. At each venue, I was met by the door guy who looked me over and then reluctantly let me come in. Sometimes I had to be very resourceful in describing what I was doing there. But I always got in, one way or another. Improvise, Adapt, Overcome.

About a decade earlier, my colleague, Frank Mix, and I were in Orlando to photograph a major convention being held in one of the large ballrooms on International Drive. A convention setting isn't like a commencement, so this was all new to us. The assignment required some time to set up two camera locations and photograph all the couples as they came in. We arrived about an hour and a half before the event was to begin. We brought our wagon full of equipment into the lobby and were greeted by an older usher, who was nice enough but firm in his resolve that we could not enter the ballroom. There was a chorus in there, and we had to wait outside until they were finished with rehearsal. "What time will the doors open?" I asked, already a little exasperated. He said they'd open about fifteen minutes before the banquet was to begin. Well, I told him that wasn't going to work for us. We had to get in there to set up, now. He wouldn't budge. We started to look for alternative points of entry. All doors locked. Frank said, "What about the kitchen?" Great idea.

"Frank," I said, "Go back out to the car and get that clipboard in the back, along with my big flashlight and my two-way radio." At the moment that radio wasn't good for anything but producing static, in that there was no one listening on the other end. We made a plan. We would enter the kitchen from the lobby egress, trying not to stop and ask for help. Frank held the flashlight and aimed toward the floor with the light on, while I carried the clipboard and squawked the radio about every ten seconds. Posted in the kitchen were some cooks and servers, getting ready for the dinner. "Excuse me," I said to the one who looked most approachable. "Can I get to the ballroom through here? Will you show me? I'm looking for something." Of course we were looking for something. Everyone could see the flashlight and clipboard. Like a soldier, the young man escorted us through the kitchen and deposited us into the ballroom. I'm sure to him we looked like the health inspectors. By now we had a small group of curious waiters who gathered to see what exactly we were looking for. We didn't give them that chance. They must have been terribly confused, but we were in. And now we could go back out the front door retrieve our equipment and set up, all while the chorus continued to rehearse. That was when Frank and I learned a valuable lesson, which we would pass on to many of our photographers over the years. When you have to get inside a venue on time, you have to find a way. If you have a clipboard, or a flashlight, or a radio, you can get access to any area you need. If you have all three, you're golden and the door keepers don't have a chance.

ELEVEN

Metering

Growing Past My Own Limitations

There have been several times over the last thirty-plus years that I've been invited to speak to groups or classes on campus about my thoughts on how to build a successful business. At the end, during the questions period, invariably, someone would ask me to describe my management style. I think there is enough in this book for the reader to have insight on what that is. I think, looking back, the more interesting question is how I arrived at what that style would be and how did I instill that culture throughout the firm.

From the very beginning, I realized that I wasn't as good as I needed to be about all aspects of business. In fact, there were some deep holes I was trying to fill in. But I also knew my strengths: I was really good at relating to other people. I knew that I had excellent rapport with the people around me. The clients, end customers, employees, suppliers, and colleagues all seemed to like and get along with me. I was a sales and service guy, through and through. I had very fine communication skills, and I could write well. And I knew, like a trainer of thoroughbred race horses, that if you gave me the right talent, I could train it to go the distance. Gail and I had already experienced great success teaching young photographers the skills they needed in the field, and when the pictures came back, we could coach them on how to do even better.

But you can't build a business based on a single strength. What I lacked at the age of nineteen to twenty was a fundamental understanding of the business of business. I was deficient in the areas of banking, accounting, finances, taxes, and risk management. But I also knew I could learn. After all, I was living on a major college campus in Florida State University, and virtually all my customers at that time were college students or recent college graduates. Even though I took some business courses, I was never going to be a banker or a CPA. I just needed some basic understanding of what I was supposed to do to be successful and build a healthy business.

It didn't take me very long, maybe a month or two, to figure out that what I needed to do was surround myself with people who were good at things I wasn't or at which I had little time or interest in becoming an expert. It occurred to me that I needed to be well-rounded, the essence of an entrepreneur. My fledgling little business was growing very fast. I needed to be out front, focused on the direction. So the solution for me was to identify really smart people with a variety of skill sets to make it all work. I began to recruit the brightest sorority members who needed part-time jobs, were reliable and very smart. They were mostly from Pi Beta Phi and Kappa Delta and almost all business majors. They, over a period of years, would run my office for bookkeeping, workflow management, product packaging, and delivery. That allowed me to focus on sales growth, quality control, and photographer scheduling and training. And I was on the road. A lot.

That goes for technology, too. I wasn't very good at evaluating new equipment coming on to the market. So our head photographer got to tinker with all the new stuff and figure out the nuances or the strengths and weaknesses of new cameras, strobes, and most importantly batteries. And when it came to computer technology, upon which we began to rely heavily in the '90s, no one in my organization wanted me anywhere near the decisions involving hardware and software. To this day, I am a self-confessed technological moron. I needed experts within my team on whom I could rely to make the right decisions. Oh, I can tell you what systems are designed to do and what the end result is supposed to be. But I can't tell you how they work. It got to the point fairly quickly that I couldn't even work in my own Production Department. I didn't know how. That bothered me for a while, but then I realized that's not where I needed to spend my time. Stay focused on the big picture. Stay focused on the goal.

As the whole enterprise bubbled up to become a profitable going concern, I began to do less and less of anything and more and more of everything. I was like a busy bee, flitting from department to department, inspiring the team and pollinating the activity. By the time Gail and I got married in 1984, (I was twenty-seven), I was doing very little in the way of personally taking party pictures at the sorority and fraternity functions. I was everywhere and nowhere at the same time, communicating the goals and protecting the values. It was just like Tom Peters taught me about the world's best corporate CEOs.

That's how Gail got hired as well.

Not only was she my girlfriend but I thought she was really bright—brilliant even—and she understood what I was trying to do. Surrounding me with young dedicated experts made sense to her. So logically she was recruited to be a trusted advisor—keep in mind she's only twenty years old at the time—then bookkeeper, then production manager, then my partner, and then finally Married To It. So in every department, I needed at least one person who was mature enough to be the expert. If they didn't have the answer, I relied on them to go find someone who did. And that meant I needed smart young women (and men). Customer service needed professional phone skills with lots of empathy, for example. Throughout the firm I needed people who possessed a solid service ethic.

I wanted people who enjoyed helping other people. The foundation of the firm, regardless of the position or the department, was to be helpful and friendly. Our mission statement became, "We help people remember the most important moments of their lives." Emphasis on help. If an employee had to leave the firm, it was usually because they didn't get it. And the ones who stayed and got promoted were the ambassadors of the idea that sales and service are inseparable.

In the graduation market, that might mean the photographer staying long after the ceremony's conclusion to take special pictures of the university staff or special family pictures for which there was no buyer. It might even mean putting a photographer in a rented helicopter because the provost wanted a bird's eye overview shot of a commencement processional through the streets of downtown Miami. "Yes sir, we'll take care of it." Do you have any idea how much it costs to rent a helicopter for a half day? Neither did I. But that's just fine. We're talking customers for life. I wish drones had been invented by 1991.

I also needed a team of experts outside the firm. The first professional I needed was an accountant, if for no other reason than to file my taxes. I didn't want any part of that internally, and this is before my accountant wife was on the scene. After a few meetings with him, Joe Sanders, he strongly recommended my next move should be to hire an attorney. I would need to transition to the status of a corporation. So now I have Dave Barrett on board who made sure we were in good standing with the State. But he was also a great mentor and business advisor. Sometimes I would book a meeting with him at billable hours to just talk. He understood what my game plan was and would offer business advice on every facet of the firm. It was like therapy. Later, that role would be filled by Belinda France.

Next came the insurance guy, Sam Rogers, whose firm we still use today. Then the banker who became very important for expansion purposes and a line of credit for the season. And finally the team included a financial planner for Gail and me personally.

The point is, running a successful business means you have to surround yourself with experts who have your best interests in mind, since you can't do it all yourself. And that realization helped me understand that, just as I was equipping myself with outside expertise, so too should I be helping grow our internal knowledge.

In hiring so many part-timers, and there have been thousands of them over the years, it quickly became apparent that we needed some formal training classes. I'm not talking about the functions of your specific job. The department heads would see to that. But I personally took on the task, with Michelle Jagers and Gail, to build a series of classes designed specifically to deal with life lessons and how each associate fit into the big picture. I wanted everyone to understand what the big picture was and how their responsibilities fit into the mission of all the other departments. Since our workflow systems transition from department to department, it was important for them to know how their actions affected others up and down the line. We called them schools. Attendance was required for all new associates. And most of the time, I would teach them myself. I wanted them to hear it from me, so they'd know what I expect. We were hiring smart young people, mostly college kids. So I wanted a high standard to be set.

Our classes included:

- Orientation School—an overview of the company, our markets, our departments, our products and services, and most importantly, the goals.
- Phone School—how to talk on the phone. It included tone and language. It is a learned behavior, one you're not born with.
- Time Management School—also affectionately known as Day-Timer school, because we gave everyone a Day-Timer to help them manage their lives. It wasn't just a calendar. Our course taught folks how to prioritize their day, their seasonal action items, incoming information, and meeting notes, and keep it all in one place.
- Packaging School—this was especially designed for the

photographers who were shipping their film and materials from the field. The value of their boxes were sometimes worth more than $200,000 in eventual sales. So protecting the contents was paramount. I was always great at taping up a big box.

I ran into Caitlyn Lennie, a current full-time associate, at a restaurant recently. Caitlin was just recently hired as a recent graduate of FSU and now works in client services. She told me that she had just finished watching a video at work, apparently made circa 1990. The video was me conducting Day-Timer school. Imagine that. Nearly thirty years later, the firm is still teaching my time management class even though they don't pass out Day-Timers anymore. It's all electronic now, but the principles are the same. It made me smile.

Eventually, when we were in the mode of refinement and fixing little problems we were having in the workflow, we invented mini-classes. These were specifically created to discuss a single issue. One I remember well was "Just In Time Production Flow." That is the idea that it is counterproductive to have one department stack the queue of the next department, and it doesn't save time in delivering the final product. Some departments actually had to slow down and feed the next department, "Just In Time."

Another was a mini-class called, there is "No Substitute For Speed." When Gail and her sister-in-law Jennifer Fitzgerald realized that our sales were directly tied to the timing of the delivery of our proofs, we tried to get faster and faster. And of course, Gail measured it every day. We attacked the bottlenecks, the impediments to maximum work

flow. Michelle led this effort, but that also meant the photographers
needed to ship images faster. We began to schedule shipping delivery
on specific flights. When we were consistently mailing and emailing
our proofs in forty-eight hours, we put in some controls to get down to
thirty-six hours, then twenty-four hours, then eighteen hours. We were
finally able to deliver proofs within twelve hours of the ceremony, a
monumental feat. Not all of them, but a lot of them. The sales rocketed.
The number of orders went up and the average order went up, too.
So we delivered our most valuable accounts first. This effort greatly
increased the value of the firm, and our potential buyers took note.
Fastest delivery in the country in this segment. Highest sales average in
the country. And it's true. For consumer delivery, there is absolutely no
substitute for speed of service. Ever heard of Amazon Prime? That was
us, way before Amazon existed.

But it was one thing for me to know how well we were doing.
For our company to be truly successful, our employees needed to know
it, too.

Every now and again, maybe about every eighteen months, I
could tell that some of my folks were feeling dejected or unsuccessful,
especially field managers, sales people, and client services folks.
Remember that I worked very hard to maintain a culture of sales.
Everybody was selling something, even internally if they were trying
to sell an innovation to the rest of the team. This applied to the sales
team trying to book new events or new schools. It also applied to client
services trying to sell new services to current clients, like way back in
the mid '90s when we began to ask current client contacts to help us

obtain the email addresses of students and parents for the purpose of online marketing. They were not meeting their goals and getting serious pushback from the clients. Email marketing was unheard of at the time, and some clients thought there was no need.

So I put together a series of mini-classes to help my folks be more successful. First was a series of classes which taught how to overcome objection, probe for hidden needs, and offer proof based on the experiences of other accounts. More importantly, however, were mini-classes designed to inspire the sales people and clients service folks who were beginning to feel like failures.

I turned to baseball. We studied batting averages. "Who holds the record for the highest career batting average?" I'd probe. "Anybody?" Staring back at me would be squinted eyes and cocked heads. A few eye rolls. If the goal of batting is to get a hit, then most players fail miserably most of the time. The all-time best career batting average is only .366, posted by Ty Cobb of the Detroit Tigers when he retired in 1928 after twenty-four seasons. The trick is to get more "at bats." Get up to bat and try again. The hits will come. You can't just quit because you're only batting .150. Improve your approach, practice your swing, and try again. THE HITS WILL COME.

We also talked about Thomas Edison and 1,000 unsuccessful attempts to create the light bulb. But he said that on the 1,001 attempt he found success. He famously proclaimed that "I failed my way to success." So I told my folks that if you're failing, adjust the method and try again. Find a sales coach or mentor. And keep trying. The hits will come. And they did. Eventually, virtually all of our clients got on board, and all of our reps were successful.

Finally, I have always enjoyed the quote by Calvin Coolidge regarding persistence (Notwithstanding creating a memorable quote, it was probably Coolidge's greatest accomplishment. Or perhaps his only accomplishment.) I am also very aware that the quote was stolen by Ray Kroc of McDonald's fame, who on several occasions took credit for its invention. But here it is.

"Nothing in the world can take the place of PERSISTENCE. Talent will not; nothing is more common than unsuccessful men with talent. Genius will not; unrewarded genius is almost a proverb. Education will not; the world is full of educated derelicts."

So I reminded my staff that the key is perseverance. And the HITS WILL COME.

TWELVE

Behind the Curtain: Life on the Road

How Not to Get Shot by the Secret Service

When my twin sons both graduated from Florida State and Appalachian State University in May of 2019, it was a moment of personal importance for several reasons. First, both boys walking across that stage and into full fledged adulthood meant, at least conceptually, that I was now the proud father of not only two more college graduates but two less dependents.

Of course, we all know it doesn't always work that way.

But, just like there's a chance that Danny and Tommy will now ascend into full-fledged financial sovereignty, there's also a chance that I may have attended my last graduation ceremony. Not a great chance, mind you. But, barring the graduation of a relative, there isn't really a strong reason for me to go. And in a way that's sad because those graduation ceremonies are as much a part of my life and livelihood as my three sons.

I've managed to attend high school or college graduations in virtually every region of this country. And my team's ideas and hands have shaped virtually every aspect of so many ceremonies around the country. Because when I was selling our company's photo services to these schools, I wasn't just selling pictures. I was selling our expertise. After all, who knew more about graduation ceremonies than the guy who was the first to photograph a high school ceremony in his state, and who had now spent more time at graduation ceremonies than anyone else in the country?

I'm happy to say that schools typically were pleased to be able to view us not so much as a vendor but as a partner. So when we offered advice, or suggested changes, they were typically readily adopted.

Basically, the success of a graduation ceremony hinges on two things: the speaker and the name reader. Most schools put genuine thought into who their speaker will be. But sometimes they take the importance of the person literally reading out hundreds, if not thousands, of names for granted. And that can be disastrous.

Think about it—the ceremony can only proceed after each name is read. And the people in the stands have traveled from far away and are sitting through three hours of hearing people's names they don't care about only to experience the four seconds of familiarity and celebration when their loved one's name is called. So that name better be pronounced correctly.

Not every school got that.

The University of Miami had a terrible reader for a long time. But that was before Donna Shalala arrived as president. In South Florida, there are all sorts of culturally specific spellings and pronunciations, and UM's reader's answer to it was to just slog through it in one monotonous transmission. I swear they could have gotten a computer to mispronounce it better.

So, being the helpful graduation ceremony expert that I was, I suggested they do what I'd seen many schools in California who faced similar articulatory obstacles do—hire a professional actor. No longer were we stuck with someone whose qualifications for public speaking were being a dean or department chair. We now had an honest to God orator, and the results were revelatory. The UM folks were thrilled and grateful to us for the suggestion.

Florida International University is also in South Florida, and though they charge much less for tuition than UM, their ceremonies were always excellent, in part because of their reader. He was a faculty member in the language department I believe, and he was the best person I've ever seen (or heard). South Florida is a very international environment, and the population of FIU was, as the name suggests, no different. Their reader knew at least six languages and was able to handle pronunciations for students who came from over 150 countries. Most importantly, he kept the line moving at a steady pace, ensuring our photographers could get the shots they needed, and the parents heard what they wanted to hear. That's really the key to an enjoyable grad ceremony. Keep. It. Moving.

Typically, the biggest impediment to a timely ceremony is the main speaker. One of the best lines I've heard a thankfully self-aware commencement speaker say was, "I know we can't start until I end." Man, that is the truth.

But I have heard some speakers do some good things with their captive audiences. Yankees owner George Steinbrenner spoke at Saint Leo University, just north of Tampa, when I was shooting the ceremony.

I was impressed that, for all his success and wealth, he came across as incredibly down to earth. A self-admitted terrible student, he made a point during the speech of noting that he had endowed everything at other universities for "C" students. As someone who himself chose to focus on things other than schoolwork while at FSU, I appreciated that.

Probably the best speaker I've ever seen was civil rights activist and former Presidential candidate Jesse Jackson. He was speaking at Bethune-Cookman University's ceremony, but he might as well have been back home behind a pulpit.

I will admit that I haven't spent much time at black churches. But being at Bethune-Cookman and listening to Rev. Jackson preach, I just as easily could have been at a revival. Most speakers engage in one-way dialogue. Rev. Jackson's was very much a two-way conversation. With calls and responses, amens, and hallelujahs, I think the crowd was actually grateful for the break of sitting through the ceremony by the time Rev. Jackson finished.

As a speaker, Jackson had been terrific. As a politician, less so. But being a great speaker and being a successful politician don't always correlate.

In 2004, Dick Cheney spoke at Florida State University. As a sitting vice president, he was a big name for mine and Gail's alma mater. Of course, in 2004, he and President George W. Bush were gearing up for a re-election, and Florida would, as it had been four years before, prove to be quite critical. I didn't care much about the politics. I only cared that, because he was, technically, the second-most important person in the country, the security procedures and protocols I had to endure to photograph the graduates were fairly arduous. Secret Service agents were all over me and my staff leading up to the event: inspecting our cases, searching our bags and bodies. Maybe I was being paranoid, but I felt like they were paying extra special attention to our team. In hindsight, I guess it makes sense. It was an election year, we were in the middle of a war in both Iraq and Afghanistan, and here was someone who was considered to be the most influential vice president in history. They were obviously concerned about his security—they even had an undercover agent wearing a robe on stage.

I just wish his speech had been better. His dry, unwavering tone may be useful in the Situation Room. But in an arena full of 12,000 people, it fell a little flat.

Honestly, I can't really complain about dealing with Dick Cheney's Secret Service folks. At least they never came close to shooting me. I can't exactly say the same thing about agents working for then President George H. W. Bush.

In 1991, President Bush was speaking to an auditorium full of graduates at the Miami Beach Convention Center for FIU, and I was captaining our team of photographers for the event. To commemorate the sitting President addressing the crowd, the university asked us to get one large image that captured the entire crowd with President Bush speaking at the rostrum. It was a fairly simple shot to get.

It would require a "Genie lift," which meant I would be fifteen feet in the air on this lift, with a large format camera, which required a blackout hood over it. Well, as you might imagine, Secret Service agents in charge of protecting the president of the United States take all sorts of precautions at public events, and for some reason they weren't thrilled about someone being under a hood behind a device that was pointed directly at the person they were tasked with protecting.

So I suddenly found myself at the center of this tension between me wanting to make sure the event was shot correctly and the agents wanting to make sure the president wasn't, you know, actually shot. And I respect that, but I also know that *I'm* not a security threat, and them keeping me from taking pictures, especially with such a high-ranking public official is a *financial threat*, so I sort of ignored their directions to move out from under the hood.

Not my best idea.

Luckily, I was able to get the pictures I needed before the Secret Service agent with what appeared to be an Uzi intervened in any meaningful way, though the agents did let me know how close I came to being the subject, and not taker, of shots.

The good news is, once you've skirted death with armed Secret Service agents, everything else just becomes that much easier. Even if it means going after a professional wrestler.

Quite frankly, I didn't know who the Rock was at the time. Dave Barry was the first speaker that day at a ceremony at the University of Miami, and he was terrific. Like his columns that started in the *Miami Herald* and then would become nationally syndicated, Barry's speech was filled with humorous lines and observations about life in South Florida. But he was drawing laughs not just with his own lines but because he kept stopping his speech and saying, "Let's hear it one more time for the Rock." I didn't know who he was, but I didn't take long to figure out that I should have his address and send him free pics from his appearance that day. One of our employees named Michael Hindman was with me that day and tried to talk me out of it. But, like with the Secret Service agents, I wasn't always the best listener.

After all—I am in charge of these events. If I saw some flowers awkwardly positioned in the middle of the stage, I would move them, knowing that they would interfere, not only with my pictures but probably the ceremony when some enthusiastic grad knocked them over. And yes, I gathered that this Rock character must be some sort of big deal (born Dwayne Johnson, he was actually an alumnus of the University of Miami and had played college football for the Hurricanes), but I was the photographer and graduation expert. And I wanted to send him some pictures.

"Bob don't do it. That's THE ROCK," Hindman implored.

"Oh yeah, watch me," I responded. "I own this."

Like I said. I felt empowered.

When I got to the top of the stairs of the stage, I looked back toward our staging area. All seven members of my staff were clearly horrified. Michael was staring at his feet and Jenn Vestal was holding her face with both hands.

I walked discreetly on stage. "Excuse me, excuse me. Mr. Rock," I whispered. "Will you please fill in your address on this card? Thanks, I'll wait."

I think it's safe to say he didn't exactly smell what I was cooking.

In the end, I never got him to give me an address. He was rescued by some Assistant Dean sitting next to him who explained we could get all that later. But what really pissed me off is that he stole my golf pencil.

The Rock is just one of many celebrities I had the opportunity to ~~bother~~ approach. One time, at FIU, I was able to get a signed baseball from Joe DiMaggio. Although attending FIU's ceremony to promote his philanthropy, Joltin' Joe was no longer signing autographs in public at that age. But that didn't stop me. I just presented the ball to him, and he beamed enthusiastically. I gave the ball to my son, Timmy who was just three at the time. For his part, Mr. DiMaggio got some free 8 x 10s.

But that's how we did stuff back then. A massive part of the Bob Knight Photo team's ethos was, just get it done. I mean we built $100 million business literally from the ground up, and much of that ground was the highways and back roads of 1980s and 1990s Florida. While Gail was in the office keeping everyone in line and raising our children, I'd be traveling with Frank Mix or Rick Chartrand or Phil LeBoutillier across the state, trying to raise our revenues. Part of our company's culture of sales and service meant being in physical contact with each client school each year, to both thank them for their business and to be able to look them in the eye and judge for ourselves how good of a job we were doing. Just because a customer didn't call to complain didn't mean they were completely satisfied. And if they had personal stories to tell us about how pleased they were, well, all the better to pass along to neighboring schools whose business we were trying to earn. I wanted to see them myself or at the least have a trusted lieutenant be there. This personal touch is, in my opinion, one of the main reasons we had the retention rate we did. We hardly ever lost a school. In fact, our numbers were so good that when our private equity partners were evaluating whether or not to buy us out, and how much we would be worth, they didn't believe us when we showed them our numbers. We were that good. But we earned it. They asked, "How many clients did you lose last year?" We said, "None."

My team and I had the state divided into territories, based on the school districts and the number of schools in each area. Sometimes when we entered into that territory, it was like a sort of special ops strike with multiple sales people in the same county at the same time. We had certain targets we knew we wanted to hit, and we would literally map them out the night before. We all had those old foldable maps, and we had to figure out where the schools were physically, how to get there, then how to get to the next one on the list. I'm not saying it was the kind of stuff Gail's old teachers at West Point would have envied, but we definitely were aiming for military precision, right down to our efforts to divide and conquer. I would take one part of the county and all the schools in it, and Frank or Rick would take another. Then we would each call on our assigned schools and try to get them to either renew with us for the following year or, if it was potential new business, sign with us. We'd do this all day, and then rendezvous at a designated spot each afternoon. Because this was in the era before cell phones, we weren't able to be in contact with one another regularly, and so adherence to our plan was essential. It seems strange to think about now in the age of constant connectedness and information, but there was a time when you didn't know where everyone was, or how to get in touch with them. Crazy, right?

Our answer to technological limitations was simple: we drank. Specifically, I mean we had a predetermined plan to meet at the first bar we saw on the right side of whatever major highway there was past the school closest to the hotel. And it had to be a full-fledged bar, not just a restaurant. We did this for several reasons.

One, it was easy to remember. "First bar, on right side of road." Two, traveling and selling all day can be a grind. You're driving all over, then going from school to school to school, then the hotel. Then get up the next day and do the same thing. At Bob Knight Photo, we always tried to make the work day as fun as possible. And so intentionally meeting at a sort of "third place" that wasn't where you were working (the school) or where you were sleeping (the hotel) I think helped break up the monotony of those road slogs. It was also about the competition. We would always travel in teams, and there was always a little unspoken competition between the team members. You did not want to be the one showing up at that bar with the fewest number of schools seen or signed. So meeting at that bar was a nice opportunity to compare numbers and sharpen each other's blades. And lastly, I'm not typically one to turn down a glass of wine or beer at the end of a work day, especially one that has resulted in new business. And our employees were typically fairly enthusiastic about Happy Hour as well. So why not incorporate it into the work day, in a way that made our lives easier?

Life on the road could be tough. It could be monotonous. And in Florida, it could be hot. And long.

Robert Penn Warren began his novel *All The King's Men* with the famous introductory sentence "You look up the highway and it is straight for miles, coming at you, with the black line down the center coming at and at you..."

I don't know if you've ever driven across Florida, but when Gail and I were building our business, we saw a lot of that black line. We would drive all over the state and sometimes at stupid times. I would have these kids working for me, and I would tell them, "OK, you're gonna go to Sarasota tonight, shoot a graduation, then go to Orlando, and be ready for their ceremony tomorrow. Photograph that, then go back to Sarasota that night for a third ceremony, then come straight back to Tallahassee."

And they'd get it done.

These days it may make a little more sense to allow team members to drive across the state at all hours of the night because they can always call or text if there's a problem, plus they'd have GPS on their phones. This was most certainly not the case when we were building our business. Our team would head out with nothing but some money for gas and a map. Luckily, they always made it back unscathed, and with our proofs or payments intact.

Not that that was always a given.

One time in the late 1980s I was down in Miami with our team to shoot Senior Class group pictures at Miami high schools during the day and then photograph graduations and proms at night. Miami is a big market, and their schools have a lot of students, and back then we would take orders, and students would pay in advance for proms and senior groups.

That's a long way of saying, between the Senior Class groups and proms, the teams ended up collecting about $60,000 in cash on that one trip. And since we were in Miami, that meant we had $60,000 in cash, plus camera equipment, in our cars. The following morning we had to go to Miami Beach to photograph one more college ceremony, and I think it's fair to say that I thought more about where my car was parked that day than at any other time in my life.

Luckily, the car was still there when we got back, and all the money plus equipment was in it as well. Back then there wasn't an easy way to deposit cash on the road, especially that much cash. Plus I would have had to reconcile it to Gail's standards.

Now all we had to do was drive $60,000 in cash back to Tallahassee and not get stopped by the police. Because, while I was a legitimate businessman, I was also a guy driving from South Florida to Tallahassee with a trunk full of cash. It tends to get the attention of law enforcement. Luckily, we got back without incident, and I went straight to the office and literally dumped all the cash on our bookkeeper's desk.

"Please go and deposit this right now," I said.

Gail just looked on in disbelief.

"You better have orders for all of that!" She knew that we did, of course, but she was just pulling my chain.

Well, of course, I had receipts and paperwork for it. I was married to Gail Knight. And for not the first time, being married to Gail might have kept me out of jail. Because the next day our receptionist hurried into our office to let us know that the FBI was in the lobby and would like to speak with us.

"Let them in," Gail told her, eyes staring directly at me.

There were two of them, and they only had a few questions.

"Do you get a lot of cash?" they wanted to know.

"For some events we do," replied Gail confidently.

"Did you have one last weekend?" Agent #1 asked.

"Why, yes, we did in fact," I responded.

"Can you prove it?" Agent #2 inquired, with not the smallest amount of skepticism you've ever heard.

Gail showed them the ledger sheets, and they told us to have a nice day.

No money laundering going on here!

We instituted a new policy after that—we would no longer deposit more than $10,000 in cash in one day. Even though it was all legitimate, we didn't want to send up any red flags.

THIRTEEN

Profitable Pixels

Making the Digital Transition

There are some industries in which success is virtually guaranteed, depending on the time you were in it. If you were in financial services in the late 1990s, for example, you probably did okay. Similarly, it would have been nearly impossible not to make good money selling mortgages in the early 2000s.

Now, obviously the Clinton era market surge was followed by the tech bubble bursting, which led to the market dropping 17 percent from 1999 to August of 2001, before being further decimated by the tragedy of September 11 that year. And the housing boom that fueled much of the post 9/11 recovery was based off of toxic mortgage backed securities, which then led to nothing less than a global economic crisis in 2008.

So the point is—industries have seasons of growth and seasons of absolute devastation. As a company, Bob Knight Photo had enjoyed significant growth for much of the 1990s. But by the end of the century, I could tell, given how technology was changing literally everything around us, we could be in for a serious turn of the tide.

As early as 1999, we knew it was coming. You have to remember, at the turn of the century, technology was both empowering and terrifying. As a society, we had begun incorporating computers really only in the last decade on a wholesale level, and then the internet had come along only in the past few years. Even the whole idea of the year becoming 2000 was threatening: we were told about the possibility of a "Y2K" glitch in which all computers and technological systems could shut down at midnight on New Year's Eve 1999 because their systems wouldn't know how to process the changing of the year to 2000.

Luckily, that turned out to be much less of a threat than we had feared. But the continued and improved functionality of computers and technology as we moved into the twenty-first century did present a major threat to our business. But also a significant opportunity.

Gail and I could tell, as digital camera sales grew from novelty spy fiction device to mainstream accessory, that digital photography was not only the wave of the future but increasingly the reality of the present. So I instructed our operations team to investigate digital capabilities. You notice I said the photographers should look into digital photography, because obviously they would be the first part of the process any digital transition would impact. In a film-based/analog environment, it was all about getting enough light on the face and on the negative, a monumental task consistently. In a digital world, it was the opposite. Unlike our first graduation at Leon, the problem was too much light in a format of digital pixels. Then, there was the fact that the image would be compressed, which also impacted the end result.

Once we got those issues sorted, the photographers were enthusiastic advocates for making the transition. For starters, what photographer doesn't love playing with a new camera? Plus, they realized how much easier life would be if and when we didn't have to reload film every thirty-six graduates. They said we should do it.

Easy enough. But I totally missed the bigger picture at the time. What happens after we take a digital image? What good is it if we don't know what to do with the image after we have it on some file in the office. Meanwhile, Candid Color Systems, our photofinishing partner was sorting out how to actually print a digital image, to make those same 5 x 7 prints we were selling to graduate families.

By spring 2002, we had the proper equipment in the field and the techies on staff were excited. New toys. We learned we could successfully capture a digital image, and Candid Color could successfully print a digital image. But we could do none of the dozens of steps in between those two events. We couldn't manipulate the images. We couldn't send the images from one place to another. We couldn't market the digital images in an efficient manner or use the internet. It almost looked like a dead end. But we knew we had to make the transition. The writing was on the wall. The digital revolution was happening with or without us.

I called it a transition in the previous paragraph, but that's really a little reductive. A transition is changing email servers or your office coffee service. What we were really considering was a transformation: a fundamental reworking of virtually every aspect of our operation, only we didn't know what we needed to do or how to do it.

Plus it would be really expensive.

Gail wanted to be cautious about all the capital expenditures or

Cap X. All that investment, she insisted, must be worth the projected efficiencies. And would that new system lead to increased sales? Not if our marketing systems, which relied on snail mail solicitations, stayed the same. On paper, the benefit to invest nearly a million dollars into a digital workflow and a new retail website wasn't materializing, at least not initially. Our team hammered it out for weeks, which led to months. By December 2002 we were ready to test our new systems in the field and in production. And most importantly in marketing.

In the summer of 2002 there was quite a bit of buzz in the office about new capabilities. But new capabilities had nothing to do with an increase in revenue. So one Monday before our weekly meeting, I went into the conference room and wrote on the big whiteboard, in huge capital letters. "It's not about how we capture images, not about how we print images or post proofs; it's about how we market images." For Gail and me, that was our new mantra.

The initial tests went well enough, though we actually shot numerous ceremonies both ways (digitally and on film), in case the digital systems proved problematic. And we still didn't have a real system figured out—the proofing system, mailing proofs, emailing proofs (totally new), capturing orders, getting the images to the lab, printing pictures, and mailing pictures to end users. All those systems would have to be reinvented in a digital environment. It scared me to death.

But Michelle Jagers saw the future in those initial test runs. She admonished us in early 2002 that if we didn't go all in on the digital transformation, we would be a dinosaur in the photography business. Is that where we wanted to be?

"A photography firm not engaged in going to a digital workflow was doomed," she said repeatedly.

And she was right. Within five years, some of our major competitors would be falling by the wayside. Bryn-Alan, the state's largest school photography firm (yearbook, studio senior photos, etc.,) closed its doors for good in 2008. They just couldn't push through. They were sold for a bargain as we looked on.

Michelle would be the project leader. From a post-production perspective, she knew what she needed from the field and in the optimum format. So she dictated how we would get grads through.

Essentially, in a period of two and a half years, we re-engineered our entire firm. Everything had to change in every department.

When we first got serious about making the change to an all-digital platform, we tried to be strategic. We were going to conjure up the best end result, even though we didn't really know what that was. We focused on systems and workflow. Every department had input, and we had meeting after meeting and hours of design sessions. It was like planning D-Day. Operations (Photography) was way ahead of the rest of the firm. So we knew we could take digital images efficiently. Then what? We finally put all our ideas about workflow together in one place and headed out to Oklahoma to talk with Jack Counts and the key managers at Candid Color. Remember, they were working on conversion plans on the back end. We figured, maybe we should work backwards or at least meet our partner in the middle. That's exactly what we did.

I remember clearly sitting in the CCS conference room, getting
started early one winter morning. The CCS team was being coordinated
through Alison Counts. She and Michelle would be working closely
together. As we watched, Michelle took different colored markers
and began to draw concepts of design on the huge whiteboard in the
front of the room. This whiteboard stretched the entire length of the
room. Michelle and Alison started on the far left side and moved to the
right. Every step in the process had to be addressed. For example, the
first step was capturing the image, then uploading the image from the
flash card to a more permanent holding location. I knew then that our
photographers were going to need laptop computers in the field. Oops,
more Cap X needed. I could sense Gail's blood pressure rising.

"How much is that gonna cost us?" she was thinking.

In the old film-based platform, we didn't need any uploading
device. We just shipped the film to the lab. But now we had to take the
images from the flash card, protect them, and distribute the images to
two different places. The full-size images needed to get to Candid Color
overnight. We then sent smaller images, called thumbnails, to our office.
The thumbnails could be sent electronically, but the thousands of full-
size images were too big to send efficiently electronically. Those images
used to actually print the eventual pictures would need to be put on a
DVD (later thumb drives). So even in this nascent stage of the process,
it got complicated really quickly.

Photographers needed to be retrained about the new
procedures. They were instructed that before they left the ceremony
venue, they needed to have the digital images in three different places

for protection. Images would need to be on the original flash card, which would not be reused. They needed to be on a DVD, which was burned right then and there. They also needed to be on the hard drive of the laptop. See what I mean? Complicated. And that was just the first step. Before we had lunch that day, that entire whiteboard was full, all the way across. A tooth-to-tail solution which would prove challenging to implement. But would it be better? I remember one of our senior photographers raising his hand in one of the training sessions to say, "Now we have to have computers in the field and burn discs? How come you're making us all jump through all these hoops?" I didn't have a good answer for him. "Just trust us, this will be better," I stammered. In reality, I had no idea if this workflow system would be better. It would take a year and a half to completely re-engineer our entire company. Every department would change dramatically.

Unlike an analog environment, in post-production, with controlled digital images, we could manipulate a single image in several different places at the same time, and we could deal with several different images in those multiple places at the same time. That meant Production, Customer Service, and Field Ops photographers all had access to all images whenever they need to see or manipulate them. This required a ton of coordination and tracking internally, but it also became a great training tool for the field, too. Whereas I had always strived to make sure every department had a focus on a culture of sales, we now also needed to make sure each employee had a modicum of technical and digital savvy. We now needed people with comfort around both customers and computers. It was a total game changer.

That also meant we now had to rely heavily on information technology to run the company. It was all about IT. Just storing all those digital images proved monumental. So we began to hire people who could write code and implement what had been designed. Then we had to update changes to the design. I suddenly found myself hiring and dealing with IT people much more frequently, which allows me to say this: As a sales guy, every IT stereotype out there is true.

When the system was in its final form, we were proud of it—so proud that we wanted to share what we had created with our client schools. We rolled it out as "Bob Knight Photo New and Improved."

As it turns out, that wasn't the best name. People wanted to know what was new, or improved, and what was wrong with what we were doing before that we needed to be new or improved?

So, we asked the marketing guy (me) and came back with a packaged system that was uniquely ours. Phil LeBoutillier, our Director of Operations and manager of the California operation, branded it "GradTrak™," and we positioned it as the fastest and most accurate Event Photography system in the world. Every other firm also had a system, but they didn't have GradTrak. We played off that for years, and the basis of GradTrak is still being used today, although much improved and much more elegant than that first version Michelle designed on that whiteboard. We first rolled it out to UCLA at a presentation, and they renewed on the spot.

A major component of GradTrak that gave us a unique advantage in the industry was in how we were able to market and sell our images to customers. We invented a system to market digital images online, even though some customers were not prepared to receive digital proofs. But what a smashing success when it came to fruition. We could now email proofs within twenty-four hours of the ceremony, receive orders, deposit the money, and seamlessly send the order to CCS without any human intervention, then we could have the pictures sent to the customer directly from the lab. And we could track everything electronically.

We learned that speed was the key. As in every business transaction, the quicker you can close a sale, the more you can take advantage of the excitement of the moment. The faster we deliver proofs, the higher the sales. So that became our obsession. And our sales people saw the benefits almost immediately.

"This digital shit is awesome," proclaimed Jennifer Fitzgerald in a meeting in the summer of 2004. Jennifer was the Marketing Director at the time and a seasoned veteran. She realized that our new-found efficiencies, increased speed of service, and greater control of our images and systems was the key to our new-found revenue. Sales had increased dramatically. All indicators were headed in the right direction, once again confirming to me that sales and service are inseparable. As she reported the numbers in that meeting, I caught Gail smiling. She knew we had made the right decision, and Michelle and crew were right in forcing the transition.

I had my own profound insights.

"You know," I said to Gail one night, "I think this internet thing is here to stay."

Because, or maybe in spite of my own ability to forecast the future of digital business trends, we were now an industry leader in the realization of the digital transformation. CCS asked if we would be willing to help some of their other customers head in our direction. We were happy to help. As long as we felt no threat from competitors/ colleagues, we were happy to help other firms and Candid Color with the conversion, step by step.

That process did several things for us, all of them good for the company.

First, it helped organically promote the value of not only our system but also our innovative ability, and that entrenched us among the CCS customers in the elite echelon. We weren't just taking and selling millions of pictures; we were solving the cutting-edge problems that helped move our entire industry into the new era.

We also were able to establish relationships with even more of the companies who were operating in other parts of the country. We knew a lot of them already from the trips and awards ceremonies Jack Counts and his crew threw for the top performers. But this allowed us the chance to get to know, and earn the trust of, virtually every other company operating in our industry. This would prove invaluable when Gail and I moved on to the next phase of the company, and it would eventually lead to several partnerships in the ultimate process of mergers and acquisitions. We called it the Friends of Bob program. And we met many of the eventual Friends of Bob in this process.

I wish I could say that when I first saw a digital camera I knew immediately that it would change our industry.

I didn't.

I wish I could say, reflecting, that when I sent my first email, or logged onto AOL for the first time (after waiting through the audible dial-up process), I knew we had an opportunity to blow the doors wide open and solidify our position in the market as experts in high-volume event photography.

But that's not what happened.

I wasn't some futurist savant who could see around corners of society and technology to position our company to take advantage of trends before anyone else. But that's never been my area of expertise. As we gained momentum in the transition, Gail saw the full potential before I did.

What we were both good at, and why we eventually did take advantage of the developing digital opportunities, was that before we invested in new computers or servers, we invested in good people.

It was our staff, as much as it was Gail or me, who could tell where we needed to go.

Michelle Jagers and others had to fight for their vision, which ultimately changed not only an industry but the lives of all the people who worked for our company.

And that is something I take a lot of pride in. Because while I never have been the most tech savvy guy, I do know people. And Gail and I hired people from all walks of life: college kids, bartenders, former business executives. But they all had to have the same software, so to speak. They had to be smart, hardworking, confident, and willing to sell. Even if they weren't interacting directly with customers, I needed everyone that worked for me to be able to compose and present a compelling case for something, especially if it was something they thought would benefit their job and, as a result, our company.

So I love that our transition as a company—from one that took pictures on film to one that took them on pixels, from one that sold via the post office to one that sold via the internet, from one that grossed a million dollars a year to one that generated ten times that—was made because of our employees' willingness to sell me on an idea.

That investment in people is one of the most emotionally gratifying decisions of my life. But it also made us lots and lots of money.

FOURTEEN

Landing the Plane

Why the Smartest Things I Ever Do Involve Listening to Gail

As we continued to grow the business and make it more profitable, Gail was always thinking about, at least in the back of her mind, what our endgame would be. I was focused on growing the business and servicing the clients, but Gail, as always, was thinking more big picture. This especially became more important as we started our family.

Our kids were born in the '90s, and colleagues asked us if we would want our boys to work with us or take over when we retired. We had never considered it. But as they were growing up, it dawned on us that we wouldn't want to force anything on them. We especially didn't want to assume that they would even want to work in the photography business, although Tim was a great and hardworking photographer for us for about five years. And, ever the numbers person, Gail also knew that the sale of our company would secure our retirement and our family's future.

I can't emphasize enough the effect that losing the Disney contract had on us and the company. We didn't really lose it. It was taken away from us by Kodak without the opportunity to fight for the contract. In the '90s Kodak was a major player on the WDW property, and as such they were able to ink a deal that gave Kodak first option on all things photographic on Disney's property. Kodak took a long look at our operation and decided it wanted in on event photography.

At the peak, our top-line revenue for Disney was $500,000 per year which was 5 percent of total revenue. I wouldn't say it was easy money, but it was seamless, and we never had to worry about it. In comparison, operating a grad season was torture. No amount of planning could make everything go perfectly, and we literally had as many checks as we had orders. Hundreds of thousands of graduates— you can imagine what a logistical nightmare our bookkeeping became.

We missed the three checks from Disney.

So here we were in January of 2000. The stock market was on a downturn because of the dot-com bubble bursting, and as a result, we got only pennies on the dollar return for the sale of our Greek business on campuses. So when grad season came around, needless to say it was all hands on deck. We were laser-focused on maximizing the income from our grad season, as that was now essentially our only source of revenue.

The results were amazing. Having all those people, our full-time staff of thirteen plus Gail and me, focused on our most profitable market had an exponential effect on our company's profit. By the early 2000s, business was still booming as a result of our efforts. Gail and our staff were constantly brainstorming new ideas to grow the size of the average order, and thus dollars per student photographed. We added a third shot to our graduation ceremonies, one before the student went onto the stage against a background in more of a posed portrait, and that increased our sales by another 15 percent.

That isn't to say those years were without their challenges. There were so many moving pieces at this time. We were transferring our entire operation to a digital format, which affected every aspect of our firm. No more film, which, you know, was kind of a big deal for a *photography company*. It also meant radical changes in how our team was structured. We needed fewer people to process and ID graduates since the digital images could be scanned and read so quickly. But that meant we needed to come up with huge investments in IT infrastructure, plus overhaul our entire marketing strategy which previously was a card containing a small proof of the physical image we were trying to sell. Now, we could just send an email. But we had to figure out how to keep people from just stealing the image we were emailing. It was terrifying and exciting at the same time.

When I look back on it, Gail was clearly the anchor of the operation. And I mean that in both a good and less-than-flattering way. Because she was so immersed in the numbers, she was able to analyze how much more profitable we were because of our focus on the grad images. But she also knew more than anyone how much this digital transition was costing, and at times she would push back against some of it. I think in her mind it might have been the AAU Junior Olympics all over again.

The digital transformation was exhausting. Gail and I had been doing this for more than twenty-five years. The balancing act between family and career was becoming more and more difficult. We didn't

work 9 to 5 jobs. It was our life and there were three young boys who
needed us too. I think Gail, as the mother, was more conflicted than I
was, but that's probably a mom thing. Or maybe it's an Irish Catholic
guilt thing. Regardless, she was thinking about how much longer we
wanted to work like this.

We also began exploring opportunities to grow our business
through acquisitions, which had proven to be a successful strategy in the
past.

A decade earlier, we were approached by Steve Counts, whose
brother Jack had helped us so much with his Candid Color business. He
wanted to know if we would consider buying his business in Southern
California. He was going through a divorce and had some other
financial issues he thought would be alleviated if he sold his business.
It would be a great opportunity for us if we could pull it off: adding
70,000 graduates and expanding our footprint to the West Coast would
increase our earnings by nearly a third.

We had never really done anything like that before, but because
of Gail, and her understanding of the metrics we were using to measure
our success, we came up with a number to buy his portfolio of clients,
which included several colleges and universities in the Los Angeles
area, especially USC, Pepperdine, and UCLA. This acquisition, and
other subsequent deals, were financed personally by Gail and me. Banks
would say they were loaning to BKP, but when a personal guarantee was
required, our names were on the hook.

Gail and I both understood that it wasn't healthy for our
personal finances to continue to guarantee the advancement of our

firm. We had to find another source of cash for acquisitions or capital expenditures to photograph more pictures of each graduate we already had under contract. We weren't under the same strain as when I was first starting my business, but it wasn't that different than when I was eating my last can of ravioli, figuring out where I was going to get the money and staff to service all these new clients.

Two things happened in 2005 that changed the rest of our lives. We invested in a small Northern California graduation firm called University Photography that required us to come up with $500,000 and we got a cold call from a brokerage firm in Chicago.

The University Photography investment was a great challenge. The deal didn't close until the spring, leaving us little time to convert their systems to ours. And the owner, Wayne Balkenhal, died unexpectedly before we photographed his first ceremony. We actually went to his funeral in April before we photographed any of the grads from those schools, which was the first weekend of May. We pulled that season off with great success because our entire team, especially Anne Munson and Frank Mix, was focused and tied into making it work.

After a very stressful but successful grad season, and experiencing the death of a colleague, Gail privately started to figure out how we would get out of this business. We had to be prepared to sell when the time was right. Whatever happened, we knew we didn't want to be the last ones out. She actually physically sat me down, demanded my full attention, and explained how exactly, when the right offer came along, we would actually land this plane.

But that would mean being prepared. If someone came calling

and wanted us to sell, we needed to know the value of our business and what we were willing to take to "walk away."

Gail had spent the past few years working at that issue. She developed a spreadsheet on the value of BKP, using the same metrics that we used when we made offers to buy other grad businesses. It was all based on the number of college and high school graduates we had under contract. It could just as easily have been used to sell widgets. At the time, we were selling two million images a year with a top-line revenue of $10 million. So, you know, a lot of widgets.

But we weren't selling widgets, we were selling systems — Sales, Marketing, IT, Photography, Finance, Customer Service. We had it all, and it was valuable to the right buyer. We just didn't know how valuable. We needed to understand the value of our experiences and our systems.

So one day, Gail's phone rang, and Virginia, our receptionist, told her that Joe Lunkes from RSM Equico was on the phone. Virginia was the best. She could spot a cold call a mile away, but she knew we usually were willing to talk to anyone.

"Do you want to talk to him?" she asked. Gail told Virginia to put him through, despite not knowing who he was or what RSM Equico did.

Before the call was over, she had committed to attending a seminar about how to sell your business. RSM Equico specialized in selling midsize firms. This basically means any company with top-line revenue of $10–$50 million. BKP at the time was barely in that range. Who knows where he got our info, but she figured it would be a learning experience. So there I was, working in the office, thinking about how to continue to expand, worrying about whether or not our new customers in California were being serviced, how our teams were looking on the West Coast, and probably a hundred other things, when I looked up and saw Gail walking into my office. She closed the door behind her, which was rare.

"We're going to Alabama for the weekend," she whispered. "I think it may be time to land the plane."

I don't remember exactly what I said, but I'm sure it was something profound and poetic like, "Huh?"

I was forty-nine at the time, and she was forty-five, so it wasn't like we were ready to retire. But Gail wanted, and in fact felt like she needed, to understand the process of what an exit strategy would look like, whenever that time would come. And I had learned long ago to trust Gail's intuition. So, we went. We made sure not to tell anyone what we were doing, got Barbara to stay with the boys for the weekend, and drove over to Mobile and went to the seminar.

Before we left Mobile, we had committed to hiring RSM Equico to sell our business. We had paid them a deposit of $50,000— lots of money for a pie-in-the-sky process at that time in our lives, for the opportunity for them to sell our business in the next five years. Just like our investment in the technological transition, we went all in, having been convinced that the current market was ripe for selling. There was a huge number of equity firms looking for investment opportunities; there were low interest rates; and there was a huge amount of private equity money sitting on the sidelines in 2005 and 2006. We also learned that our business would be more valuable if Gail and I stayed involved, which for us was the best part since we weren't really looking to leave the company. In addition to a cash buyout, we still could maintain our strong salaries. It was having our cake and eating it, too.

At least that's what we thought.

Committing to starting the process of selling was the easy part, but there would be a thousand details to overcome. Gail spent the next six months documenting the financial history of BKP, down to the most minute details, and projecting out our revenue for the next five years. What resulted from that process was a Confidential Information Memorandum, or a CIM, better known as 'The Book."

This book is what Joe Lunkes put out into the world of equity firms so that he could gin up interest in BKP. And boy did he. Beginning in September of 2006, Gail and I started to meet with various potential equity partners so that they could determine if they were interested in making an offer to buy our company. To be honest, it wasn't until we started to receive offers that I realized this was a real thing. I was actually generally opposed to the idea until I started to see some numbers with lots of zeroes on the end.

One of the hardest parts of this whole process for us was the secrecy. Nobody knew what we were doing. NO ONE! Gail and I were having these clandestine meetings with private equity firms at the University Center Club at Doak Campbell Stadium or in the Atlanta airport and having to lie about where we were going and why we were spending so much time out of the office. Our staff knew something was up, but they didn't really press us. I think it's because they knew we had their backs. They knew we wouldn't make a decision that wasn't in their best interests. But it didn't make not including the people with whom we shared everything any easier.

We were interviewed by twenty different organizations. But it wasn't just them interviewing us—like a pledge at a sorority, we were interviewing them, too. In the end, we chose Raymond James Capital out of Tampa, Florida. It was a tough decision, but we clicked with them, and both of us agreed it was a good decision. I think the fact that they were Florida-based helped them in the end because BKP was a Florida firm, too. I liked how their chairman, Dave Thomas, was totally focused on us and treated us the way I had trained our team to treat all of our clients.

Around this same time, we learned that Chappell Studio, our biggest competitor and the company with almost one million grads under contract, was also going through the same sales process we were. RJC was going to make a play on them too. But another New York-based private equity firm we had interviewed, Friend Skoler, made it clear that although they weren't the firm we chose, they were going to have a presence in the event photography space. Upon the recommendation of Joe Lunkes, RJC formed a partnership with Friend Skoler, and both private equity firms moved forward as a new joint entity. Event Photography Group was born, and we reinvested in the new entity.

That was Thanksgiving of 2006. The next three months would be like nothing we had ever done before. The reality was that we had no idea what we had just gotten ourselves into. We had literally been wined and dined by RJC, but now we had to prove ourselves. This process, commonly called due diligence, reminded Gail, the Irish Catholic girl, of confessing all your sins to your local priest. Except this time Hail Marys were not going to work. If we couldn't prove that BKP was as profitable and efficient as we claimed, it was going to cost us money.

Most of the burden of due diligence fell to the finance crew, which in those days was Gail, Martha Mitchell, and a bunch of part-timers. They had their work cut out for them, but I knew they would come through. They were all smart, hardworking, and had the best leader possible in Gail. Martha was a trooper—working lots of weekends leading up to Christmas and then after the holidays. By this time we had pulled the entire full-time staff together to tell them what we were doing. Once again, it was all hands on deck, which was nothing new to our staff. Gail and I were so focused on making this work because we knew that we had to prove the true value of our firm. The private equity guys were looking to give us a haircut.

In the world of private equity deals, a "haircut" is a reduction in the offer price for the firm, usually due to some variable that the acquiring firm disputes. The concern might have an effect on projected growth or revenue going forward. Think of it like a buyer negotiating a lower price on a house after getting the inspection. It's pretty common, we had come to learn, that getting a "haircut" was more the norm than not.

That variable for BKP was sell through rate, or simply the percentage of people photographed that actually make a purchase. The history for the grad business was that about 40 percent of the grads photographed actually bought pictures. Our projections for growth showed that due to improved marketing strategies, we predicted an increase to almost 43 percent by 2010.

Well, the guys at RJC completing the due diligence process thought otherwise. By this point, almost 70 percent of our sales came in online, and Raymond James disputed our projected increase in sell through rate because national web-based businesses were showing a flat sell through rate. So other national websites' inability to raise their sales figures was going to cost us almost $1.5 million. They also said that the deal wouldn't be as valuable if they couldn't acquire our competitor, Chappell, and implement our systems with their clients and end customers, who was usually mom.

Now Gail is pretty passionate about a few things: our sons, good wine, and the sales metrics at our company. So she took it personally that they were questioning them. She had been spending about twelve hours a day crunching different numbers for weeks. When the word came down that they were offering us a "haircut," it would be safe to say she lost it.

I should mention that our attorney, Belinda France, was with us from day one. She was our attorney, but she was also our counselor. I remember her coming to the house one Saturday and almost physically pulling Gail away from her laptop. Gail was driving herself crazy trying to offer up counterevidence to Raymond James's projections. Obviously, saving $1.5 million in valuation was important. But for Gail, it wasn't just financially motivated. It was her reputation on the line.

Just as selling the Greek party pics portfolio of business had been tough for me, because it was something I took so much personal pride in, this was Gail's moment to struggle with the overlap of her personal and professional identity. After a quarter century running these numbers, she had become Married To It.

But Belinda could see what Gail was doing to herself. And she was right. It was time to step away for a few days.

For Gail, a few days meant basically a few hours. And it helped. Stepping back made Gail realize, and I agreed, that we owned a very valuable asset. We didn't *have* to sell at that time if we didn't want to. We were putting close to a million dollars into our brokerage accounts every year. We were doing just fine. So Gail told Belinda to tell RJC that we were going to walk away from the deal.

Remember, Gail is Irish and tends to have a hot Irish temper. So it's either black or white for her. On the other hand, I try to be a little more deliberate and nuanced in my approach. It's why Gail and I work so well together. She's the numbers person: it either works or it doesn't. I am sales and service: if it doesn't work, there is an adjustment we can make somewhere to get us to the finish line.

I knew that RJC needed us to make EPG's investment in Chappell work. It was easy to do the math. Chappell had one million graduates but only averaged about fifteen dollars per grad photographed. Our average was pushing twenty-five dollars per grad. Implementing our systems with their customer base meant an increase of ten dollars times one million, or ten million dollars right to the bottom line. It was a no-brainer.

I was up all night the day before Belinda was to meet with RJC and tell them we would be willing to walk away. I literally paced the entire house, thinking about what the sale would mean to Gail and me, our kids, our extended family, and the people we worked with, who were essentially all part of our family as well. I didn't want to walk away from the sale, but I also didn't want to accept less than full value for our business, and I sure as hell wasn't about to tell Gail and our team that I thought their numbers were anything less than sterling. Finally, around 4 a.m., I came up with an idea: we would take the haircut at the closing of BKP, but when we closed on Chappell, we would be paid the difference, and we agreed to reinvest that additional payment into the new company. Skin in the game. We wanted a chance to share in the growth of our new company, Event Photography Group.

Our partners went for the deal, and we closed the sale. BKP was sold to Event Photography Group in March 2007 for $18 million, plus stock in the new organization which made Gail and me the largest individual stockholders. We were also given two of the six seats on the Board of Directors of the new entity.

We actually could have closed sooner, but we had to wait for BKP's thirtieth anniversary trip to Grand Cayman. Gail and I always wanted to reward our team and their spouses for their hard work and dedication. In September of 2006, BKP was thirty years old. We needed and wanted to celebrate, but we were in the middle of the negotiations and legwork that the sales process required.

We got the idea of taking a trip to the Cayman Islands after we had gone to a Candid Color seminar in Miami the previous year. When we planned the trip, I had no idea that our new partners would have a problem with it. We were paying for it; they weren't. But apparently, the fact that all of our full-time management team was flying to Grand Cayman on the same flight had them worried. They also didn't want to give us a big fat check right before we headed to the money laundering capital of the world. So we didn't close until we returned safely back to Tallahassee, crew intact.

EPG closed on Chappell Studio in May of 2007, and we reinvested some of our proceeds, including the extra $1.5 million they tried to shave off our heads. We were off and running to consolidate the market and create the largest event photography firm in North America. Gail and I were still involved, but we would have a new boss and new colleagues. It would be the start of another challenging but equally profitable adventure.

FIFTEEN

Meditations on Merger

Our Business Acquires a New Mantra

The day Gail and I officially became multimillionaires, after consuming a fabulous dinner, we spent the night at the InterContinental hotel in Buckhead, Atlanta. After returning from our trip to Grand Cayman, and with Raymond James being satisfied we were still alive and able to help lead our business into this new era, we closed on our official sale on March 7, 2007. We thought the transition was going to be great because we were going to be the primary go-to people in the new firm. We would not have to be in charge anymore—I would not have to be CEO, and Gail would not have to be in charge of the numbers—but everyone would still be coming to us for advice, and we were still going to tell everybody how things should be done. We were confident.

Within a week that confidence was gone. We realized quickly that, to borrow a phrase, we weren't in Kansas anymore. In fact, we would soon be in Iowa.

But we might as well have been in Oz.

Fairfield, Iowa, was home to not only Chappell Studio, one of the country's largest event photography companies that we acquired

that May but also the cultural home to the philosophical movement
known as Transcendental Meditation, or TM. Pioneered by Maharishi
Mahesh Yogi, TM was the practice of meditating twenty minutes or
more a day. Given notoriety by celebrity practitioners like the Beatles in
the 1960s, the movement took over America's heartland, literally, when
in 1974 the Maharishi purchased Parsons College, located in good old
Fairfield, and created the Maharishi University of Management, which
required its students to study TM.

The original Chappell owners were from Chicago, and
they specifically moved away from Chicago to be closer to the TM
movement. They moved their entire operation and their families out
there. Then, they started to recruit people from around the country who
wanted to be closer to the movement to work for Chappell. Not to put
too fine a point on it, it was not dissimilar to a cult.

Many of the Chappell employees were TM people who had
moved to Fairfield. All of the top-level management, probably the top
twenty-five people, were all what was known amongst the locals as
gurus, or "roos." Then, everybody else—all the worker bees, the ones
that were paid ten dollars an hour—were called "townies," because they
were from Fairfield, but they weren't part of the movement. All the
desks in Fairfield were required to face east. And they had a meditation
room just off the lobby so that at any time you could go in and meditate.
Maybe even levitate. (Another townie nickname for the "roos" was
"floaters" because of their belief in the ability, through consistent and
disciplined meditation, to levitate.)

The first season for grad shoots was actually taking place before

EPG officially merged its two wholly-owned subsidiaries, BKP and Chappell, so we were able to just execute under our existing BKP setup. But we were still on the hook for performance. All those projections for Chappell's portfolio that I vowed to correct, Gail and I needed to pull off. There was a lot of pressure. We didn't let the fact that it was no longer our money affect the work ethic we put into our performance and sales and marketing.

By that summer, Chappell had shot their portfolio of grad ceremonies, and we had shot ours, and now it was time to begin thinking about the integration process. Of course, Chappell was much bigger than we were, but much less efficient. The two companies were vastly different in how they operated, which made the process of how to integrate complicated. The results were different, too. By midsummer of that year, the board decided that somebody would have to be CEO of the new merged company. It could not be me. As longtime rivals for grad business, Chappell and BKP had too much bad blood between us, so they needed an intermediary CEO. So a former Kodak executive named Paul Rasmussen was tasked with taking over the new company and leading the effort to blend the best of both worlds into one new, highly profitable universe.

Because of our superior metrics in terms of profit per graduate, we expected the intermediary to merge the BKP systems into the Chappell portfolio, but that is not what he did. He looked at Chappell as the larger company, and he thought it would be easier to just use Chappell's systems for certain things, and we would use our systems for these other certain things.

It was not a wise decision. But the price for the new money in our bank account was that we were no longer calling the shots anymore.

But that didn't make it any easier to accept.

The stark reality of what it really meant to not be CEO anymore came in July of 2007 when the new CEO said to me, "Listen, this practice of us running around and visiting all the schools once a year, we're not doing that anymore."

I said, "What?"

What I really wanted to say was, "Are you an idiot?"

"Unless you're a certain level of customer," Rasmussen explained, "we're just not even going to go see you. And, if they don't sign their contracts, we really don't care."

I was horrified. It was a slap in the face to not only me and my relationships with all of the customers we had serviced over the years but also to our entire philosophy of sales and service.

But again, neither Gail nor I were in charge anymore.

They gave me a title. I was the Senior Vice President of Sales and Marketing, which was logical, but they basically put zip ties around my hands, especially if as VP of Sales and Marketing my team and I were no longer going to be visiting schools. But we continued to visit our clients any way.

At BKP, we always did a college tour, and we saw every school. We didn't care how good a school or bad a school they were in terms of their number of grads or our profit from the account; we saw almost everybody. There were some exceptions. Maybe there would be one or two smaller high schools, like Madison High School or Marianna High, both in the panhandle of Florida, that we did not go visit, but other than that, we saw everybody. Chappell didn't see anybody.

Chappell had a grading system for ranking their client schools. They assigned each school a level, sort of like Delta Sky Miles. There were diamond clients, there were platinum clients, there were gold clients, and then there were silver and bronze clients. To use technical sales-speak, bronze clients didn't get shit. Silver clients didn't get much more.

The new CEO wanted to apply that rating system to our portfolio, and the software was going to drive the sales effort that was made for those schools based on their rating. The rating was, for the most part, based on gross revenue.

The rating system created a self-fulfilling prophecy. A gold school was never going to make high enough revenue to be a platinum school because they didn't have enough grads, even if they were making ten or fifteen dollars more per head than a platinum school. All the schools that were rated as diamonds were the schools with the most students. For example, Trinity School in Orlando is just a small private school with about eighty kids. But we were grossing $4,000 a year from those eighty kids. That is fifty dollars a head almost, which was an extremely high number for us. But to Chappell, and for the newly created Event Photography Group, Trinity would be a gold school, which meant it barely got any attention at all.

Rollins College, also in Orlando, is another great example. It is not just private; it is elite. A liberal arts school with a lot of money, most of the students are from the Northeast. Rollins has a huge endowment,

but they only had 350 grads. However, their dollars per head was
something like forty-five dollars. It is a great account. In the Chappell
system, they got shuffled down and rated gold or silver just because they
only had 350 grads.

As much as I tried to explain that schools with such a
high dollar per head yield were worth the personal touch, the new
management didn't get it or care. So schools like Rollins stopped getting
much attention, if any, from the new team.

As a couple who had built their entire career on customer
service, that was a slap in the face. But it felt like a gentle pat on the back
compared to what we endured with our new computer and database
management system.

As everyone got more comfortable with the merging of our
firms, the decision was made to integrate departments separately—
Sales and Marketing first, then Production and Finance, then Client
Services, Customer Service and Operations. The departments from each
company were working together, but their computer systems were not
integrated. Some tasks were completed in the BKP system and some in
the Chappell System.

The last piece to fully integrate the two subsidiaries would
be the IT Department. IT had to be the chain which connected
everything. If the chain were to break, systems and workflows in several
departments would be damaged.

We thought Chappell's IT system was awful. Some of it looked
like the code was written in different decades. But everything they had
was tied to it, so management thought it should stay.

And in some sense, the decision was understandable. Chappell's owners were IT gurus, literally, and they wrote all the software they were running. So there was no doubt that Chappell's leadership had more IT experience than we did.

But, like their spiritual philosophies, it was based on an older system.

Our system, GradTrak, was based on a seamless solution from image capture to final print delivery. It was based on a partnership with our photofinishing house, CCS. But management ultimately forced us to put all of our client information into their database in Fairfield.

The results were literally a disaster.

We began the integration process in February of 2009. Well, with the grad season coming up only two months later in April, it was not enough time. Michelle Jagers kept telling them it was not enough time. She made it clear that it was not enough time to get all the bugs worked out before we shot the first grad photo. We didn't have the systems ironed out, department to department. And she was right.

Part of the problem was that Chappell made their digital conversion later than we did, and they left several holes in it. It wasn't a complete system. We lost images. We lost addresses. We lost sequence. There were no longer proper internal controls to keep all the information together. We were literally losing some flashcards with images on them because people in the field didn't know what to do with them or were reverting to old habits. We couldn't get our hands on them, so we were delayed in posting proofs. Those proofs that should have gone out on May 15 didn't go out until July 15. Well, that destroys everything, because the highest sales are the ones that are closest to the ceremony. So if you wait three months before you mail your proofs, your sales are going to be diminished by 50 percent. And they were. You have to remember that we are talking about millions of images from thousands of schools. Not every school was a problem. Not every photo team was deficient. But enough mistakes were made that summer of 2009 to put an enormous dent in our year-end projections.

We were a photography firm. If we lose the images, then we have nothing to market. If we lose the addresses or the sequence, even if we have the images, then we don't know who is who. Then we found out that the marketing system was also flawed. Some of our emails weren't getting to the customers. We found out in late summer that some of our emails were not going through to the recipients because they were being designated as spam. All told, our new company, which combined for $35 million in revenue, burned through $5 million in profit because of our problems. It was all fixable, but we were going to have to work fast to recover and tighten our controls. In the BKP Tallahassee office, none of us had ever worked harder or been more demoralized from the setbacks of this integration.

Rasmussen chose the Chappell system over the Bob Knight system because Chappell was the bigger company. And truthfully, the people running the new company didn't appreciate the true value of what we had developed with GradTrak.

Chappell was also really top-heavy on employees. Gail noted that they had ten people in Finance just chasing their tails, not doing any of the stuff that was really important. We had fifteen full-time

employees, including Gail and me, and they had 100. Their Customer
Service Department was top-heavy. Their Finance department was top-
heavy. They even had twenty people in IT.

Some of those people were just there to check on other
people. The former owners of Chappell did not trust their employees.
They were paranoid, so they would spy on them through their IT
Department. Everything was backwards. They made everyone clock
in. They wanted to measure how much time each person spent in the
office. At BKP, we didn't care how much time people spent in the office
as long as everything got done. Our employees knew what to do. Under
this new system, it was helter skelter. We had merged with the most
archaic company that we could. The only thing that they had was huge
numbers. But when your systems are bad, big numbers can mean big
problems. And that's exactly what happened.

Everything that could go wrong did go wrong, and it was awful.

Even their system for measuring our progress was flawed. Their
computers had the capability, but it was all misguided. They were
measuring all the wrong things for all the wrong reasons. They kept
ten people in their finance office to job cost every invoice that came in,
which meant that in the season, you would get a $50,000 bill each week
from the post office on postage for mailing out proofs. They wanted
us to then go in and divide and designate that $50,000 into separate
accounts for each school. Well, that wasn't how Gail handled expenses.

What Gail did instead was to say—hypothetically—we spent
$50,000, and we mailed out 250,000 proofs, so that's twenty cents
a grad, so she applied twenty cents a grad in her spreadsheet to tell

whether a school made money or not on the cost of mailing proofs. Chappell wanted all actual costs allocated to each individual school. Gail knew that the big costs, actual photography pay and travel expenses, needed to be charged to each school. But most of the other costs could easily be allocated based on a formula.

Also, in the field, we had long-time Chappell photographers, along with long-time BKP photographers who were shooting in the field. We had different cultures. Our standard was we're not going to miss anybody, and their philosophy was, well, get as many of them as you can. Then, we started to put our teams together, like you from Bob Knight are going to work with you from Chappell. They didn't get along. They disagreed on how to do things. So sometimes when materials from a ceremony arrived in the office to be sorted for post-production, we couldn't tell what to do with it, because the Chappell people weren't following the new rules. They'd say, "You know, I've been shooting grads for twenty years, and you're not going to tell me how to do it differently." It was almost like they were sabotaging the systems we were trying to install. So, some of those people had to leave.

In July of 2009, they decided that all the key players involved in this merger would fly to St. Louis because that's where Paul Rasmussen was, and that is where his corporate office was. Gail, Michelle, and I spent three days in St. Louis with a consultant to try and figure out where all the holes were. It was a grueling three days. When we were headed back to the airport in St. Louis, the line to check in at Delta was really long, and all we wanted to do was get through security and get to a bar, because we just wanted to go home.

This was when Delta had just merged with Northwest Airlines and had essentially taken over Northwest's operations.

The line, and the experience of the other customers, was clearly not going well. We finally get up to the ticket counter and Gail asks, "What's the deal here? Why is this taking so long?"

The woman at the counter looked up at us with her brand-new Delta uniform. Obviously, she was a former Northwest employee who was trying to figure out all the new systems at Delta. This was her first day at that ticket counter. This was only one day after Northwest had officially gone away. Everybody was wearing Delta uniforms, whether they knew what the hell they were doing or not.

The new employee, with frustration in her voice and exasperation on her face, asked us one question.

"Have you ever been through an integration?"

That's all we needed to hear.

"Take your time. It's fine," we all said. "Whatever you need for us to do, we're happy to do." And we all just backed off. With that question, she called off the dogs. Because we were three pit bull customers, coming up to the counter and about to jump her shit, but then what she said made a personal connection with us. It was good business. And it was good for us to be able to experience from the customer side what we had been dealing with as a corporation.

The other positive from those meetings was we realized we had some support from the Raymond James people, because they sent people from Tampa to check on how we were doing and reported to the chairman of the board about what they were seeing. One of the guys who was trying to help fix everything said, "You know, the difference is that Bob Knight Photo had no IT Department but a tremendous IT vision."

He added, "The difference is that Chappell has an IT department with absolutely no vision."

That helped the management realize who should really be running the show. So Gail started spending more time in Iowa to help get their systems in line. She was going up there one week a month for like six months. Finally, she put her foot down and said, "I don't want to do this anymore." They said, "Then make a plan to move it all to Tallahassee," and she did.

We specifically invited some employees to transfer. They could come to Tallahassee, and we would have a job and a space for them. A few of them transferred but not many. A couple of the employees that moved down from Fairfield are still working in Tallahassee, specifically Caroline Capper, who is now Production Manager. But the rest of them were adamant that they were not going. That was their choice. Paul Rasmussen and I told them they had thirty days and thanked them for their service. We had to rebuild whole departments in Tallahassee. To some extent, that was successful, especially Finance and Client Services, because I was running Client Services and Gail was running Finance. It was like the old days.

But there were still massive problems.

Because we had two different systems for production, and Michelle had her hands full, some of Chappell refused to change their systems so that we could get the freaking images through the lab. So that all ended up on Michelle's plate.

Of course all the problems, including the decrease in sales, didn't go unnoticed by the board. So when they asked Paul Rasmussen about it, he did what a lot of deficient leaders do. He blamed someone else.

Since Michelle was running point on integrating all the new systems and setting up the new office in Tallahassee, we perceived Rasmussen thought he could pin any systemic shortcomings on her.

Luckily, Kris Hansell from Raymond James offered some support. Kris had been the one who had done the due diligence for Bob Knight Photo and Chappell Studio. So he knew all the people who worked in the offices. He probably knew them better than anybody.

He drove up to Tallahassee, and he got right in the trenches with Michelle's production troops. He was learning what the problems were, so he and I had this long conversation in the parking lot of our building. He just said, "You know, she's doing everything she can, and she is being thrown under the bus." So he protected her as much as he could. And eventually the board replaced Paul Rasmussen as CEO. Michelle, with the help of a newly appointed CEO and the rest of the managers, was able to help lead us to a full IT integration and get everyone on one platform in all departments.

After that, we got back to smooth sailing. And, with the power of the wind from the new national portfolio, our ship was making excellent time. The profits of the new company were tremendous, and for the next few years, Gail and I learned to navigate the waters as first mate, rather than the captain. I mean, the money was good, and since we were now all in Tallahassee, we felt like we could at least keep an eye on the wheel, even if we weren't technically steering it.

But then Gail, always mindful of the numbers, saw a way for us to make even more money, though it would involve a decision, and actions, that would prove to be amongst the hardest of my career.

SIXTEEN

The Second Bite

My Life as a Subordinate

From Day One, we knew that there would be a second sale, because that was the only way that Raymond James and Friend Skoler, our new partners, would ever get their money out of it. The goal, always, was to make money. Doing a corporate merger is very much like flipping a house. You want to buy it low, then add value to it along the way, and then get out of it before any major problems arise, hopefully selling it at a substantial profit. Hopefully a double-digit percentage of increased value. Our partners told us they usually cashed out of projects like ours after about seven years. But, regardless of the timeline, the goal was to make sure that the value of the firm was greater than when they first invested in it. So we got very busy, very quickly, at growing the firm.

The first step was to take Chappell's portfolio and monetize it more effectively with our systems and metrics. As I just discussed, this was much harder than we anticipated it would be. But after years of wrangling, and after finally relocating key personnel to Tallahassee, we felt like we had that massive ship headed in the right direction. With our systems in place, and Gail's ability to put the focus on the right things, Chappell's portfolio became more valuable pretty quickly.

That was good, but it wasn't going to get RJC, Friend Skoler, and the two of us where we wanted to be. Part of what made buying our firm so attractive was the vision we had laid out to our investors that our metrics and systems would improve the performance of any other firm out there. Chappell had been a great first test case, and a massive one at that. But we knew it would work for other photo firms as well. So we set about the business of buying out other companies, located around the country, also doing business in the commencement segment, only not as efficiently or lucratively.

Back in 2006 in the early negotiations with Raymond James, we actually put together a spreadsheet of potential firms we could acquire to let them know what was out there, and what we should be going after. It wasn't too hard to figure the assets or the value of the portfolios of the smaller firms because they were all regional.

We called it "The Friends of Bob." I mean, many were actual friends who were looking to get out. And some were companies that had struggled in the digital era and could see the writing on the wall.

In fact, I don't think we would have ever gotten the deal we did without our spreadsheet of the FOB.

The first close on our first deal was in April of 2007, right after EPG was officially formed. It was a small deal in Arizona, and that owner, Doug Wyland, still works for us today. We've known him for thirty years. He was our first one, which was good for us because it proved to our partners that we really could deliver on what we said, that we really did have friends out there who were willing to vouch for us.

We understood that the only way to make money on our

investment in the new firm was to execute on these other acquisitions and implement our more profitable processes and systems.

Bob Knight Photo, reborn as Event Photography Group, was averaging, between the high school and college portfolios, about twenty-four dollars per graduate photographed. Most of the firms that we bought were between twelve and fourteen dollars, and some were as low as ten dollars. That's why we were so valuable to Raymond James and Friend Skoler. So we bought up these firms, modernized them, and monetized them.

We made them use our same websites, implemented the GradTrak system, and started taking and selling second and third pictures during ceremonies: a closeup and the one that's posed after they get off stage. We also put a premium on fresh, personal email addresses from all graduates and parents. Then our Client Services Department began collecting cell phone numbers of the graduates so we could text them to let them know that their proofs were ready for viewing. Another marketing game changer. Part of what made us as successful as a firm was that we were offering some things that a lot of other firms weren't: gift items, plaques, a frame with a tassel, etc. We were always trying to think of and test things that parents of graduates would want to buy, that would give us a competitive edge on which we could make a big margin. And, of course, we were tracking these things because of Gail, so we could confidently go to any prospective firm, see what they were charging and making, and know that we would be able to increase the profitability significantly. And that's exactly what we did.

We did fifteen different deals in the commencement space

alone, and the new company was taking shape. We bought up firms in fourteen states, including Texas, Washington, North Carolina, Colorado, South Carolina, Louisiana and California that added an additional 400,000 graduates to our portfolio. This was on top of the 1,000,000 grads we acquired with Chappell. So with our twenty-four dollars per head rate, we had added over $30 million to our revenue stream.

And as our business was growing, I was also growing. No longer a CEO, I wasn't really in the photography business anymore. I was now in the mergers and acquisitions business. And I was getting good at it.

Once again, I have to say that we were quite fortunate to be in the mergers business when we were. EPG was born in 2007 when the economy was riding that late George W. Bush economy high. Of course, that would change dramatically later that year. But for the time being, the business was ripe for growth. And we were taking advantage.

Not that our colleagues and competitors from around the country were thrilled about it.

"You partnered with Chappell?!?!" more than one of our friends and fellow photography company owners said. They were both hurt and jealous. We all saw Chappell as the evil giant we were competing against, only now we had thrown a saddle on him and were riding it to our retirement. And that left others looking up at us.

We would go to the same seminars we had been going to for forty years, but suddenly we weren't at the center of the social circle. Bobette had turned into Hester Prynne, and our Chappell money was our scarlet letter.

Being perceived as a villain can be tough. Especially when its people you've known and lived life with for thirty years who are now thinking of you in a negative way, as a Benedict Arnold.

But it can also be quite profitable. And that was before we figured out how to maximize the profits from digital images.

In the era of physical film, every professional photographer would do everything they could to protect the negative. You don't get rid of the negatives; you don't sell the negatives. You sell everything else, but you don't sell the negatives. Above all else, that tiny foundational image was sacrosanct.

Well, when we got into the digital era, some of the people that we acquired didn't pick up on the fact that the best sale of all is when you can sell a big package of prints, and we'll now include the digital images, for an additional fee. At first it was a disc we would mail, then we would email the images, and now we just give them a link to a digital download.

So, from a real dollars standpoint, being able to just wirelessly transfer digital images that, other than the software that produced them, cost us practically nothing, was very impactful. Our profit margin was huge, because we were selling single images for forty bucks, or you could get them all for sixty-five or seventy, and the cost to us remained minimal.

God, I love this business.

The margins were so good on digital images that some in the company wanted to sell them exclusively. "We'll sell the digital images only, no prints," they argued to me. "I mean, after all, our margins are so much higher."

The problem was, and still is, that the perceived value of any digital image decreases every day.

Our average sale was seventy-five dollars in 2007, but if we moved to exclusively digital images that number was going to go down, because nobody was going to pay seventy-five bucks for three digital images.

That's why we had to have a mix, and our customers told us that they wanted a physical memento, mostly to display in the home. It didn't need to be big. We're not making wall portraits, but they wanted something to display in the house to show the accomplishment of that moment. And, of course, if the graduates had siblings, the parent would have no choice but to have pictures of both of them in their house. So we were not in favor of ceasing the sales of our physical prints. In fact, 60 percent of our customers said they wanted something to display in the house, and I think, for as much as we now exist in a digital environment for social media, that's still the case today.

But, of course, if we can add the digital images to the mix, that's even better. So the other thing that we learned that is fairly consistent, is that 70 percent of the buyers are women. We started to track that very carefully. And in the high schools it's all women, because it's all moms.

We only knew that most of our customers were women because of our extensive surveying efforts which, while being very informative, were quite costly. You could spend a quarter of a million dollars in a hurry trying to figure out what's in the head of a parent of a grad, or the grads themselves. What we found was that, especially on college campuses, if we could get their eyeballs on our images while the family was still together, our percentage of sales went up significantly. Which makes sense: if the graduation was on a Saturday morning, they have the images in their email inbox by the brunch on Sunday morning, and maybe the mom or rich aunt is three mimosas into it, and she goes, "Oh yeah, let's get copies for all of us."

We love rich aunts.

That's why twenty-four hours was so important, because they were together, and then they look and see that the pictures were available, and then they could look at them together. Most importantly, whoever the decision maker was could make that decision before they left town. If we got the images delivered within twenty-four hours, it meant as much as an extra ten to fifteen dollars per graduate. And with the size and scale Raymond James was expecting us to achieve, that would become very real money.

But the key, then, was getting the email addresses and cell phone numbers.

Sometimes you get the school to provide it in the file with the students' addresses, or we would pass out cards and get them to fill out the cards with their address and email address on it. At least 95 percent of schools use a name card to read as the kids come across the stage. So what we would do is tell our team that it was incumbent upon the photography team to go through the line and make sure everybody filled out that card. And be relentless about it.

I mean I've got a business I'm trying to sell. Again.

When we started it was like religion: you better get the damn addresses before you come back here. But for the Chappell folks in 2008, it was more like Sunday School. They only did it about half the time. Plus, they relied solely on what the school provided. They didn't try to go out and add any additional information. Well, we learned early on in our careers that for the information the school had, at least 20 percent of those addresses weren't correct. Schools might be good at many things, but keeping accurate contact information for their students wasn't among them—especially in colleges, where local addresses change by semester.

A lot of high school addresses proved to be inaccurate, too. They just got rolled over from year to year. Whether it was error, divorces, or moving, the records we got from high schools would have put me and Gail in the poor house. The most accurate system that we would have would be getting them to fill out their address at the very moment that they're going to graduate. We had a lot of information that we were collecting off that card, and as long as you kept the cards and images in sequence, we could meet our email deadlines. It made it so much faster. We were getting our proofs up and in the customer's email within twelve to eighteen hours. Once we acquired Chappell and their additional million graduates, the time frame extended to twenty-four to thirty hours. And damned if, with each additional marketing email we sent, we weren't adding more money to our bottom line.

But our equity partners still wanted more.

I mean, I was out there signing up these firms, almost prostituting myself to my formerly good friends, and then I would call up the bosses at Raymond James and Friend Skoler to happily report on a new acquisition or other positive development. They were less enthusiastic than I was.

"You did your job," Dave Thomas would bemuse. "What do you want, a medal?"

One time, I was on the phone with a prospective new firm when Dave called.

Our receptionist buzzed in with the news. "Tell Dave I'm on the other line, and I'll call him right back," I told her.

When I called him back, he let me know that I should take a different approach in the future.

"Bob, before we begin, you need to know that when the chairman calls, you take the call," he said. "And everyone has a chairman."

I didn't love having a boss.

Before we were bought, Raymond James already had a vision of how big we could get. By looking at the "Friends of Bob" spreadsheet, they estimated what we should be worth after five years before we were even bought. Of course, acquiring other companies meant we were changing our business model. Not only were we now in the corporate merger business but we would exploit two more event photography segments, including Santa Claus and endurance race photographs (marathons, bike races, triathlons).

Raymond James and Friend Skoler always talked about the need for three legs on the stool. We were in the grad business, and we had acquired from Chappell a sizable portion of the marathon race photo business. That's 150 marathons per year worldwide including five of the six World Marathon Majors: New York, Chicago, Boston, London, and Berlin. The third leg of the stool for EPG was a different type of endurance event: Santa Claus and Easter Bunny pictures in 400 malls throughout North America.

Raymond James knew from previous research that the Santa and Easter Bunny mall picture business could be quite lucrative. More than any sentiment for holiday pictures, though, Raymond James knew that if we acquired the mall business, we would become the $100 million top-line firm that we wanted to be. Then we would need to operate that successfully for two or three years at that level before we could cash out for good.

But running a company that takes pictures of toddlers on the laps of people in costumes can bring its own challenges. Gail and I both were so focused on the grad business, so everybody's job was grad related. When we acquired Marathon Foto, we mostly had everyone in silos. You either worked for GradImages or you worked for Marathon Foto, and then once we added the Santa portfolio, you were part of the mall team. We soon realized how inefficient that was. We were never going to turn around the Santa Claus and Easter Bunny numbers unless we got some of our systems into that market.

Enter Jen Fitzgerald, our sister-in-law, who was, and in fact still is, in charge of consumer marketing.

Jen is married to Gail's brother Paul. So you see, Gail and I weren't the only ones Married To It.

For years, Jen's job had been related to any product marketing that went out of the building: the website, what we offered, the pricing, all aspects of the customer experience for grads. Well, all of a sudden her job changed, and now she was doing it for Grad, for Marathon, and for the Easter Bunny. Just like Anne Munson, who also now was in charge of operations for not just graduates but races and screaming kids all over the country. So it changed people's jobs tremendously.

That was a transition, but now when I look back on it, it worked really well although there were some rough patches when we were first doing it. And when people got those different positions, they got a little bit more money, but they got a ton more responsibility.

And it was a completely different world. You know when you take your kids to see Santa, it's all done on-site. And you have no idea who is showing up, unlike at a graduation.

The Santa Claus and Easter Bunny business became popular in the '60s and '70s, and the model did not change until we started changing it. They were doing the same thing, every year for forty years. Their margins weren't that good, and the problem with the mall business is that people think that the malls do that themselves, and of course they don't. They contract it out and take a huge cut off the top. (The malls typically wanted 50 percent of a photography company's take.)

Neither the marathon nor Santa Claus markets were nearly as profitable as the grad markets. As our partners put it, their contribution to EBITDA, (Earnings Before Interest, Tax, Depreciation and Amortization) was far less significant.

The grad business had 95 percent or more of the contribution towards earnings, and the mall business and the race business had about

2 percent or less each. It wasn't hard to figure out that we needed to turn all of our attention to a renewed focus on the grad market, the one that's making money.

But the point wasn't the profitability of those companies. It was about the top-line numbers and for us to be able to show we had grown from a $10 million a year business to one that brought in over $100 million. It was about making the pie bigger to attract larger firms into a partnership with EPG. Acquiring those other two segments allowed us to do that.

That was the benefit. We wanted to show somebody that, look, we took the company from $10 million to a $100 million, and that's why we're valuable, and we're still growing. That was our hook to get people's attention for the second bite. And then once somebody bought us, they would probably split it up, which would be smart to revert to specialization.

Denise Conroy, the new CEO of our firm, which was renamed Iconic Group, plus the administrators of Raymond James and Friend Skoler were the ones managing the sale process of the firm for the second bite. Gail and I didn't really have a lot to do with it. We were just at the table, albeit with black chips in the pot. Everybody in the firm knew that we were starting to look at the sale process. Our seven key holdovers from Bob Knight Photo each got 4,000 shares of stock in the new company. Our sponsoring partners gave us those shares to incentivize our team to stay on and keep working hard. Then several of them got more shares for different things over the years. So they had chips in the game, too. But the job was to keep this company running and showing profits and growing so that we would be more valuable. That was where we were. That was our job.

Ultimately, we really took the advice of Dave Thomas. From the equity side and from the investment company, we really trusted his vision. So when he said it was time to get out, we listened. We were the largest individual stockholders of the firm. The other stockholders were largely investment firms, so our lives were the ones most likely to be impacted by this process. So when Dave Thomas said, "We're all getting out, and this is the play," we were relieved. We didn't want to stay in because, on the off chance that this didn't sell, we didn't want to be stuck with this thing for the rest of our lives with the investment that we had in it. We were thinking that if we didn't move soon, we were going to miss our opportunity because no one knows what's going to happen to professional photography. And the truth is, we still don't.

We were actually ready to sell in 2014, which was seven years after RJC bought us. In fact, we started to get really nervous. Like bank robbers watching their partners linger in the vault with cops on the way, "Let's go, come on, let's get out of this thing," we would say to one another. But Dave Thomas and Steve Skoler weren't there yet. They thought that we had to grow it a little bit more, and we had to demonstrate consistent profitability for years.

They knew there was still more to get in the vault.

Finally, in late 2017, they emerged with large sacks of cash in both hands. "It's time," they said.

Thank God.

Instead of being seven years, it ended up being eleven years, which, for an equity company to keep a company for that long, is unheard of. Those equity firms would like to have their money out sooner as well. So they were trying to make a good decision about not being too long and not being too short, but they were calling the shots. All we could do was advise, but when it came down to it, they made all of the decisions. They were really smart. Our two partners never came into a room to talk about anything unless they were already in agreement. In other words, there was never a time where we were the deciding vote, because the decision was already made before they got to the room.

In the end, we emerged, thanks to them, with another significant payday. And not just us: our full-time employees in Tallahassee who had been granted stock in the new company in 2007 ended up with five figure Christmas presents as well. A nice thank you for their help in managing, among other things, Mall Santas.

For us, the work of Dave and Steve underscored what I think I learned that first day, in my old apartment, as I freaked out over my last can of ravioli. Your business is only as good as the people who work for it. And I couldn't have asked to work with any better. I mean, Gail and I loved our employees, just like we loved the business. How else do you think we ended up Married To It?

SEVENTEEN

Fading View

Invest in the Brand to Protect the Brand

E arly on, before we had an identity or an official brand, I struggled with what this business would become. Who were we and what was our mission? What exactly do we do? Sure, we photographed sorority and fraternity parties, and we dabbled in the commencement business. But who were we?

As BKP became a corporation and registered with the state, I tried to evaluate what we would become. At the time in 1979, we were shooting everything. If it would stand still long enough for my flash bulb to recycle, and it could write a check, we shot it. We had our fledgling commencement business, and, of course, back then the Greeks at FSU were the centerpiece.

Dave Barrett, our first attorney, and Belinda France, our current attorney, were valuable mentors. Dave had said, when we were first incorporated, that I was now the owner of a viable entity that could only be destroyed by the Department of the State, or the courts. I was grateful that we hadn't been a corporation when I was kiting checks to the post office.

They understood what we were doing in those early years and

put the pieces in place to successfully protect the firm from outside threats, which thankfully never came, and focus on the imminent expansion.

Dave Barrett said, "Focus on your firm's strengths. The way to build a small business is to find the one thing you're really good at doing, and then try to do that one thing better than anyone in the world."

Wow.

It may seem simple, but that crystallization of what my mission was or should be was really helpful. In the end, what did we do really, really well?

Let's see: We were really good at Party Pics and other event photography opportunities. We shot thousands of Little Leaguers in youth sports. For that, we used the same marketing system as that first Leon High graduation. Which is to say, not a great one. It was pure speculation. We had no guarantees of revenue and were shelling out cash before we knew how much, if any, we would be recouping.

So in 1981 we settled on what our mission at BKP would be. We were exceptionally good at event photography—specifically, taking and delivering large volumes of pictures for large volumes of people.

Our mission, written for the first time in that year, would be, "We help people remember the most important moments of their lives." But how we did that was by focusing on the volume. Volume at low prices.

We became the McDonald's of photography. Which, you know, wasn't the worst business model.

We weren't a photography company, one of our corporate suitors would say. We were a logistics company that happen to sell photographs.

That required sophisticated systems built to service thousands of customers at a time. You need a wedding photographer? That's not us. You want a family portrait? I'll give you some references. In fact, we didn't have a pricing schedule for brides and a single wedding would have been a burden on our systems. We didn't know what to do with a wedding. But if you need someone to take 14,000 pictures in a single night at Disney's Grad Night, or you have 5,000 graduates crossing the stage on May 10 and you need all those images mailed out in thirty-six hours, well, I'm your guy. Our business was built on systems to handle large volumes. That's what we do. That's our mission. It still is. And selling that mission, and our ability to execute it better than anyone else in the world, was what got me up and out the door every single day.

There's no doubt that our company achieved the success it did because of the motivation and execution of our incredible team. It was that original BKP team in Florida and California who were all on board in the late '90s up until the sale to Raymond James and Friend Skoler. They are the ones who engineered and managed the conversion to an all-digital platform and GradTrak. This is the team we want to recognize in this book

So here they are: Michelle Jagers, Anne Munson, Jennifer Fitzgerald, Rick Chartrand, Ryan Gay, Frank Mix, Damien Byrd, Jen and Jason Vestal, Martha Mitchell, Fernann Yozviak, Carolina Swanburg Summers, Sandi Donlevy, Michael Hindman, Phil

LeBoutillier, Christina Copare Evard, Theresa Bell, Kerry Wilson, and Virginia Sawyer.

They were all laser-focused on the vision and values that Gail and I projected for the firm.

I think there are a few reasons for this. One was because Gail and I worked every day to make sure the team was motivated and empowered.

That's one thing I don't understand these days: I see more companies bring on new salespeople and give them a guaranteed salary for their first few months while they train, but no commission opportunities. To me, that's exactly backward if you want a motivated and highly performing staff.

Now I understand the logic of it for a potentially poor salesman: come in, learn how to sell, and don't worry about starving while you make your way. But what if the new hire is motivated and savvy? You're directly disincentivizing him from going out there and busting his ass.

I mean, when are you more motivated to do well in a job than when you are just starting out?

I used to try and think of ways to give new people more commissions. When I gave new reps territories, the first responsibility I would assign them would be to go out there and re-sign each school in your area. If you did, you got a bonus. If you were then able to go out and sign up a new school, you would get even more money. I feel very confident about the fact that our sales were as good as they were, and our people were as motivated as they were, because of how we structured their bonus opportunities.

But all the motivation in the world doesn't matter if you can't sell. So everyone we hired, regardless of the position, had to be sales-oriented.

One of my favorite tactics to use when I was interviewing potential hires, no matter the position, was to make them sell me something. Sometimes it was my tie. The best candidates, the ones we hired, would find something about it to mention to me.

"It looks really good on shirts like yours. The colors look great."

"This model makes it much easier to tie three different types of knots."

"It works for any kind of date. At dinner...or in the bedroom."

We didn't hire everybody.

Sometimes I'd make them sell me my pen. And what I was looking for was basically the ability to close. Tell me about its features; then ask me something to force a decision.

"So as you can see, you won't be able to do your job effectively without this pen. How many will you take?" someone that got hired might've said.

Someone we didn't hire might've offered, "Uh, you don't want to buy a pen, do you?"

They might be working at the actual McDonalds.

I don't get to sell much these days. Maybe that's one reason I'm writing this book. I want to sell people on the best way to do business, based on the tremendous success Gail and I have experienced. And I just don't see too many people doing it this way anymore.

My son, Tim is a salesman now for an adventure travel company. As you might expect, I have offered no shortage of input: some solicited, much not.

I know Tim will be successful. Not just because he's Gail's and my son, though I'd like to think that will help. But I know he wants to do well, and he's got the skill set. Plus, I've made him sell me my pen on more than one occasion.

I still have one of those pens. Frank Mix, in fact, recently gave me one he had hung onto after nearly twenty years. It's an old-school swivel with an emerging tip and strong ink flow. The body was red, and it had "Bob Knight Photo" written in our trademark cursive, which we patterned after Disney.

Frank pointed out, with no small amount of pride, that the pen still worked.

I'd like to think that means something. I'd like to think that Gail and I made sure that anything that had our company, and our family's, name on it would be quality.

I'd like to think the pen, like our sons, is proof of that.

Acknowledgements

Building a business can be challenging. As we've learned, writing a book about building a business is a different type of task. And we couldn't have done it without the following people:

Jack Counts, Our Mentor and the one who helped us most, especially in the beginning.

Dan Hays who helped us realize as we grew, that we should trust our managers to make their own decisions, as long as we thought their hearts were in the right place. The power of empowerment.

Linda Coe - confidant, supporter, cheerleader and travel buddy

Our 3 Boys, Tim Knight, Danny Knight, and Tommy Knight. Thanks guys. It's been a family thing all along.

Our Parents, John and Cindy Fitzgerald and Edwin and Margaret Knight. You made it all possible and brought us up right.

Barbara Long, a huge part of our lives since 1987 and the glue that held our home life together.

Belinda France. Our trusted advisor, attorney and very good friend.

Eric Eggers, who has spent the better part of the last two years helping us get the whole story down on paper for this book.

The original BKP management team of the late 90's who revolutionized our business in 2003 with a new digital platform. Special thanks to Michelle Jagers, Anne Munson, Jennifer Fitzgerald, Phil Leboutillier, Frank Mix, Fernann Yozviak, Rick Chartrand, Ryan Gay and Martha Mitchell.

Neva Kidd, Gail's college roommate who, along with her co-workers, coordinated our largest and most important commencements for more than 15 years.

Damien Byrd, the cocky point guard from Port St. Joe High who became the most beloved associate and most dedicated manager in the firm.

Paul Fitzgerald, Gail's brother and Bob's brother in-law and best friend, who started at age 16 and was Head Photographer for several years.

Sandi Donlevy, Carolina Swanburg Summers, Theresa Bell and Carla Beisheim Levine who all came in with guns blazing and took a chance on us when they had more valuable options. They gave us more trust than we deserved in 2004-05. 15 years later Carolina, Theresa and Carla are still with the firm.

Jenn and Jason Vestal who fell in love on company time, became two of the best operators and photographers in our industry.

Doug Wyland, a lifelong colleague, the first acquisition of the "friends of Bob" and the only previous owner still working for the firm.

Christina Copare Evard - Campus Coordinator and Field General for a decade of Disney Events.

Mike Mendez, my first roommate and by default my first photographer and office assistant.

Marlene Hagen. Bob's first full time associate who worked out of Bob's apartment.

… And Michael Hindman